Not Plain Sailing
VICTORY

A novel

L.J. BERNARD

This book is a work of fiction; names, characters, places, and incidents are either products of the authors imagination or have been used fictitiously. Any resemblance to actual events, locales or persons, living or dead, are entirely coincidental.

The Author acknowledges the occasional use of New Zealand place names and wants to address that she may have never been there, and they have been used fictitiously.

Originally published in 2025.

All copy rights are *reserved with the author*. No part of this publication may be reproduced, stored in a retrieval system, or transmitted, in any form, or by any means (electronic, mechanical, photocopying, recording or otherwise) without the prior written permission of the publisher.

ISBN 978-0-473-75439-6

Cover design by 'Get Covers'

Books by L.J. Bernard

The Journey Trilogy

Insurmountable *Faith*

She Finds *Love*

Not Plain Sailing, *Victory*

To my fantastic, much loved children,

Meghan and Christopher.

May you be blessed with the right choices in life,

may you be wise, happy and supported

by all the people who love you.

Lots of love from mum.

To all my friends and readers that continue to encourage me,

your support and wonderful comments are an inspiration and

very much appreciated.

Thank you.

Not Plain Sailing

Victory

A love story of

Determination and triumph.

You can face life's problems with either fear or faith, Fear will focus on the storm; faith will focus on your inner strength.

Isaiah 41;10   Fear not for I am with thee, be not dismayed for I am thy God; I will strengthen thee!

....

Happiness is not the absence of problems but is the presence of Jesus.

2 Timothy 1;7   For the spirit that God has given us; along with power, love and self-control.

....

Philippians 4;13

I can do all things through Christ which strengthened me.

Chapter 1

Gemma's gorgeous Labrador dog Wilson has moulted golden hairs all around her lovely cottage by the sea, and as she pushed the vacuum cleaner with great gusto under her queen sized bed, the pretty cream bed spread printed with multiple pastel coloured flowers fell in soft draping over the sides of the bed. She pondered how Wilson's short hair could find their way into so many nooks and crannies and she felt a little irritated by it today. The brush on the bottom of the metal tube caught on something, not to be beaten she tugged harder and wiggled the cleaner impatiently and out came a large white envelope.

She hadn't looked under the bed since she moved there three years before and had forgotten that she had eagerly flung things under the bed in her rush to settle in, making this her new home. Picking it up jogged her memory, she stepped onto the off switch of the vacuum cleaner with her slipper-clad foot to douse the noise. Suddenly curiosity made her unable to resist, she reached in to have another look at the legal application to divorce her husband Mason Brownlie and the attached decree nisi which was granted in what seemed like someone else's life a very long time ago.

At the time of speedily unpacking her possessions and finding a place for everything, Gemma hadn't been sure where one would put something like this important document in it's spectacular white envelope. Evidential proof that must be kept, although something that she preferred to disappear completely from sight and mind. When she moved there she was an emotional wreck seeking peace and wanting to begin again after her marriage to a sick husband where she suffered domestic violence and grief, a world of torment that at the time she thought would prevent her wanting to be with any man ever again.

Gemma sought peace and made a new life with the company of her lovely dog, a world away from her past. And once she had emotionally healed she began to see her dance partner in a new light.

She started to date Jonah Frederick, he was a strong, muscle endowed farmer with brown eyes a depth that she found she just melted into, endowed with tanned skin from long days spent on the land with deer, cattle and farm maintenance. Jonah was fun, kind, sincere and hardworking, his thick greying hair and dark rimmed reading glasses wrongly suggested a business side to him; being in his sixties and only a few years older than Gemma. With patience and understanding he won her heart as she slowly learnt to love and trust again. She sat on the bed looking down at the large envelope and considered how her life had changed, the extremes never ceased to amaze her and she knew it had been God's work. A look of wonder filled her eyes with a sparkle of excitement as she remembered those times long ago compared to now as she has a wedding to plan, something she never expected to happen in her future.

The phone in the kitchen rang out, interrupting her thoughts and any idea of vacuuming, she throw the envelope onto the bed and rushed towards the phone, it would be him.

"Gemma, when are you coming around?" Jonah asked impatiently.

"Ha ha," she laughed. "It's only Wednesday, I thought I'd see you on Friday and stay the weekend, what do you think?"

"I can't wait to see the prettiest blue eyes and feel your soft brown hair again," he says, "So why don't you come around later today and wander around to check on how well the orchard we planted is doing?" he was speaking softly, seductively.

Laughing she replied that she was busy doing housework and jokingly added, "Won't the orchard be there on Friday?"

"Shall I buy chocolate." He asked.

"Yeah, that might work, you know I can't resist chocolate. I won't stay over though just pop in for a while later on okay?"

"Sure, see you later love!" Accepting that's the best he'll get.

"Bye darling." Hanging up the receiver just as Wilson came running in and sat beside her. He had been outside, not tolerant of the vacuum cleaner noise she had been making.

Looking down at the official document still on the bed, she patted him and began to chat.

"Well, I might need this information later when I get married eh Wilson." Taking it to the office she had set up in the spare room and finding a drawer full of receipts, she slipped the envelope in there making a mental note to remember where she had put it.

"We probably have time for a walk to the beach after I put this vacuum cleaner away in the cupboard. Do you want to go to the park?" His big ebony eyes cheerful along with excited snuffles and full body wagging she presumed that to be a yes.

Clipping on his lead was a breeze now he sat nicely and had matured to 18 months old, and she could see him trying to restrain his excitement in his attempt to keep still. Lifting the strong leather lead away from his worn collar they began to proceed down the driveway. They both loved going for a walk beside the road to the beach with its long expanse of white sand, often lined with black and white oyster catcher birds fossicking amongst the clatter of shells as they pecked for food. There was no dawdling today as she longed to see Jonah. The fresh breeze blowing salt air stung Gemma's face as it arrived in sharp gusts from the sea.

Meanwhile back on the farm, Jonah discarded his farm overalls that reeked of stinky silage he had been feeding out to the deer and cattle. He wanted to be in plenty of time before he heard her car rattling over the cattle grid which crossed the beginning of his driveway. Gemma pulled up in her faithful little Honda car. Jonah rushed off to put the jug on and grabbed a block of chocolate from the top cupboard, part of his secret supply he stashed there last week to spoil Gemma with, he quickly slid it onto the kitchen bench as he scampered to open the front door for his lady.

Gemma always insists on her independence and neither of them have a key to the other ones house. Arriving in front of Jonah's garage door she parked the car and let Wilson jump down off the back seat, he sprinted up to the front door which was already just a little ajar and pushed his noise inside.

"Hi, I'm in the kitchen making tea, have you had a good day?" called Jonah as he heard the door squeak and Wilson and Gemma both head for the kitchen.

"Hi darling, nothing special just housework, and we went on our regular walk to the beach and park of course, looking down at Wilson as he ran off to find a toy to play with. Wondering over to Jonah the deliciously sexy smell of musky aftershave permeates the air as she reached up to wrap her arms around his neck and time stood still. He bent his head to kiss her while at the same time firmly wrapping an arm around her waist, pulling Gemma in, she felt so totally comfortable and safe with him.

"What have you been doing today darling?" She cut in, trying to act normal and not let him notice how physically attracted she was to him.

"I had some farm work to attend to in a couple of paddocks with the tractor, I have thirty head of deer in each and the grass is getting down a bit now so I gave them extra feed. We desperately need some rain to make the grass grow." He says while his mouth snuggled into her neck. "Where do you want to have your cuppa?"

"Outside beside the spa will be nice eh. What's happening in the orchard?"

They sat at a long marble slab table on comfy armchairs covered in soft outdoor fabric under the tinted plastic roofing, the glare of the sun had started to go down in the west becoming a nuisance, so thank goodness the roof created a very pleasant relaxing scene with the moist ferns and green pot plants around the spa pool.

"Oh, you'll love it, I've been watering the trees we planted and the citrus are getting some scented flowers on them now, plus a few of the boysenberries are ready to eat. The grape vines are putting on a lot of growth and I want your opinion on the Tamarillos, they look terrible." He said with a thoughtful smile.

"Okay, Wilson can have a zoom around while we walk about and have a look at how it's all going. Are the animals all doing okay?"

"Yeah, a few of the cattle are ready to go to the works, they're huge." He declared proudly.

"Gosh, be careful then." Suddenly a rush of concern for his safety cut through her.

"I'm always careful around the bulls, you never turn your back on a bull, and there is one that I'll get rid of as soon as I can, I don't trust him, he weighs around 600-700 kg now.

"Oh my goodness, that's dangerous."

"I've been handling them for a long time, I know how to manage them don't worry. There is another one that I think will be difficult to load when the truck comes as he could break down the holding pen if he's spooked, but the truckers are pretty good though." he says.

Looking lovingly into Gemma's eyes he spoke quietly, "Anyway now you've accepted my proposal I wondered when we can go and get an engagement ring. It's something that's been on my mind and that's really why I was insistent on you coming around." He smiled.

Gemma's face instantly lit up and the warmth of happiness ignited inside her, like a rose bud opening to create a breath-taking visual display, she was radiant, life was perfect.

"Oh yes please, can we go tomorrow and visit your mum afterwards so I can show her my ring? My daughter Bridget will be home after 2pm so can we go there after your mum's place on our way home? Then you could phone your sister and I'll send a message to my brother in Australia and my son Carl." He was busy working in the South Island of New Zealand. Gemma was exuberantly joyful.

Jonah broke a row of chocolate off for her to munch on while they strolled around the orchard holding hands with all the time in the world. Handing it to her before picking up the other hand and softly gripping it to provide balance for her as she stepped into sturdy gumboots and they headed out the back door. Wilson knew the way and was one step ahead of them, he loved to run around behind the high windbreak and dashing in and out of the rows of trees was also fun for him.

"That's a great idea, of course we can." He was smiling at the excited babbling Gemma was doing.

Jonah's hand was warm and comforting, wrapped protectively around Gemma's as they stroll along examining all the new growth and looking to see what needed an extra tie or stake. They bend to pick the fruits of their labour collecting a little handful of raspberries and boysenberries off the almost thornless vines, eating the berries along with the chocolate tasted divine, a mixture of luscious fruit, cocoa and yummy sweetness. Standing still to eat and soak in the warmth of the New Zealand sun they were both aware that now early March it was nearing the end of summer and there had been the occasional mornings they woke to dew covering the paddocks. As they quietly walked together peacefully contemplating, the grass clippings Jonah had placed around each mandarin tree was letting off a pungent damp smell challenging the sweet aroma of the orange and lemon blossoms, blending with the quietness of trees happily growing alongside the sounds of livestock snorting around over the fence, life felt so good now they had each other.

Waking the next morning Gemma was aware of a blend of excitement and nervousness knotted in her stomach, it's Thursday morning and she is going to look for an engagement ring, but how much should she spend? Nervous at how to carefully broach the subject before they go looking, she felt a bit awkward about spending his money.

Leaving Wilson with a nice fresh bone taken out of the freezer last night, Gemma settled him in the back yard of her cottage and explained she won't be long, before heading off to see Jonah. He's already up and dressed just having a coffee as she arrives at his home and she decided to sit outside while he finishes it. His outdoor area around the spa pool is beautiful and she took time to admire the giant stone urns full of lush ferns, sitting behind the polished stone slab with rows of chairs tucked tidily under each side, the bright rays of morning light just appearing over the fence a short distance from the house while the strings of tiny lights wound around the steel poles supporting the roof always came on just after dark. Sounds of water gently bubbling in front of a backdrop of hard stone behind the aqua blue spa and trickling down over stones that were also surrounded by ferns and peace lilies with their stately spires of white flowers, it was a tranquil setting and round concealed lighting had been inserted at the base, shooting their rays of light upwards illuminating the green fronds further creating calm and mindfulness.

"Are you ready to go then?" Jonah snaps her out of this blissful moment and back to the excitement of why she was there.

"Yes, I can't wait." Her heart was pounding from the thought of a new ring and her insides all a flutter with a thousand butterflies.

"Let's go." Gemma leapt to her feet and headed through the garage door to the parked car, he had several but opted for the new electric Kia Niro Hybrid for shopping trips. Driving along the road it was as though he could read her mind as he started to ease any concerns.

"When you see a ring you really like, I'm happy for you to have it, this is the last engagement ring you'll ever have so you have to be happy with it okay." He insisted.

"Okay, and I'll make sure the wedding ring fits around it nicely for later on eh." She smiled back with relief.

"Good idea, you want them to match and sit well on your petite fingers." Jonah smiled nodding as he drove.

They both found that driving alongside the paddocks on rural roads was always enjoyable and it didn't take long to arrive at the shopping mall which housed three very renowned jewellery stores. They took time to have a good look through all three and then headed for a frothy hot chocolate and carrot cake to talk about which one was the nicest.

"Well, I know that I want yellow gold and diamonds." Gemma explained as she thoughtfully narrowed it down in her mind while speaking out loud.

"Okay, do you want a big solitaire diamond or a cluster?" He asked smiling, his face full of wonder, he seemed to be really enjoying her struggle to decide.

"I'd like to go and try that one on again, you know the one with the diamond and gold leaves curving around it with the small diamonds on each side." She draw around her finger pointing.

"Yes, I liked that one too, and the wedding ring matches and isn't just a boring band of gold. I want you to have something special." They were both in agreement about that!

"Let's finish our drinks." She said impatiently as she couldn't wait to go and get it! Jonah laughed and was enjoying every minute of her conundrum.

After slipping it onto her finger for a second time she know that was the one. The girl behind the counter explained she would get it resized to fit Gemma's petite finger, which would only take about 30 minutes if they could come back.

"Oh, that's great, we'll just go for a look around and will be back soon, thank you so much." Gemma was pleased and had the biggest happiest smile ever. Jonah went over to the counter to pay for it while she wandered off outside. She didn't want to know how much it cost.

They wandered around looking through the many shops and only the women's clothing stores could hold her attention as all she could think about was the elegant engagement ring and wondered at how fantastic her life was since buying her home at a breath-taking beach that she loves, found an affectionate little dog and met Jonah, every day was a gift now.

    Returning to the store, it was ready waiting for her in a gift box and paper wrapped with a pretty bow on the top, thanking the salesperson they walked out hand in hand, Gemma had the biggest smile in the entire mall.

Chapter 2

Sitting looking at the little red box nestled in her hand, Gemma sat back in the warmth of the car holding it tightly, content with a smile on her face. Jonah affectionately looked over from the drivers seat and asked if she wanted to wear it to show his mum. Without answering she opened the lid and carefully removed the precious ring from its box, she slipped it onto her finger. Stretching her fingers out in front of her Gemma looked admiring it, while Jonah quickly glanced over, it fitted perfectly, with a grin she silently approved.

"Are you all set to go to mums to show her?" he asked.

"Yes, let's go," she whispered, nervous but excited. "Do we need to phone her first?" enquired Gemma.

"No she'll be home; she doesn't often go out now dads gone."

Gemma had only met Violet a few times since going out with Jonah. He visits and takes care of his mum's finances, visiting her once a week. She was very difficult to take out now with poor mobility, so Jonah's sister Pamela usually took her to do any shopping she needed; Violet usually waited in Pamela's beautiful new EV outside each store.

Jonah turned into her old, cracked driveway, which was lined both sides with pretty hydrangeas, they had just finished flowering. Gemma noted that they needed to have all the dead heads cut off and knew that Violet often asked the lawn mowing person to tidy her garden for her. She was hard of hearing and didn't hear the car arrive, Jonah banged rather loudly on the door. As Gemma and he stood waiting, they could hear her pushing her walking frame and crashing into the skirting boards as she slowly made her way to the frosted glass front door.

"Hi mum," uttered Jonah, as the door opened. "An unexpected surprise for you with an extra visit this week."

"Oh, that's nice." She said solemnly and apathetically.

"You sit down and we'll make ourselves a cup of tea, do you want one?" Jonah enquired as he gave her a hug and they headed towards the kitchenette.

"No, I'm fine." She dropped down rather heavily into her recliner chair.

After returning from the kitchen with two cups of steaming tea balanced on saucers, Jonah carefully placed them on the dilapidated coffee table and they both took a seat on the well-worn sofa. Looking at each other, Jonah couldn't wait any longer and swiftly announced their engagement. The two of them were bubbling over with excitement, and Gemma hurried across the small room to the recliner to show Violet the beautiful gold and diamond ring.

Violet never looked up at Gemma as she talked over her, nodded and told Jonah. "It's very nice."

Leaving Gemma rather disappointed and silent at being ignored, her enthusiasm was crushed and in no doubt unwelcome, she longed to escape back to her refuge by the sea. Her special exuberance was obliterated as Gemma reasoned that Violet resented her seeing Jonah more than she does or didn't want to share him. Who knows! But the whole time over their cup of tea Violet never looked her way or spoke to her. No congratulations or smile. With the coldness Gemma began to wonder if it was worth getting into another relationship or was it just too upsetting. She didn't linger as the atmosphere was tense, so after the tea was quickly drunk Gemma placed every ones crockery into the dishwasher and they all hugged and said goodbye. Climbing into Jonahs car without speaking they drove away from his mother's house, Gemma was quiet, disturbed that Violet was not pleased for Jonah to marry, and also a little shocked at her rudeness.

Jonah is 65 years old and has never been married, Gemma now wonders if it's because of his mother's loathing, putting doubts in his mind, perhaps making him feel responsible for her now that she's on her own. Violet was in her eighties and will inevitably die, leaving Jonah alone, with only one sister who has her own life. Consoling herself, she had wanted everyone to feel as happy as they both did.

Jonah didn't seem to have noticed that Violet ignored Gemma, she was quite rude, how could he not notice? It seemed to confirm her suspicions that Violet had snubbed other prospective daughter in laws.

"Let's go and see Bridget, she'll be home from work now." Jonah suggested as he pulled out of the driveway with a wink and a quick glance across from the steering wheel. "I'll phone Pamela tonight."

He chatted away while smiling, either he didn't notice his mother's vulgarity or was pretending so as not to upset Gemma, on their special day where she was taking a step that at one time, she thought she would never want to do again.

A twenty minute drive with her mind questioning how her daughter Bridget would take the news. Pulling into her driveway they're greeted with a lovely newly painted picket fence, Bridget and John proudly upgrading their new home. This was something they have worked on together, and Gemma started to well up. It's so lovely that they do stuff together and make memories. She was still getting over the disappointment of Violet not being happy for her and Jonah. Looking out of the side window she quickly blinked away the tears, not wanting to upset Jonah.

Bridget looked happy but surprised to see them as she waved and smiled from the kitchen window, they both climbed hesitantly out of the car and went to slide open the ranch slider, unaware of what reaction they would receive. Her daughter was pleased to see her, the emotions now a turmoil of enthusiasm whirring around in Gemma's stomach as she was reservedly excited again.

"Hi, are you just in from work?" Gemma called to her and reached for a hug.

"Yeah, this is a surprise, I wasn't expecting to see you, are you out shopping?" she enquired.

"Well, we have some news to share with you and we have been out shopping."

"Oh well, I'll put the jug on." Bridget says looking concerned.

"I've decided to say *Yes* to Jonah's proposal." A smile spread across Gemma's face as Bridget turned to fill the electric jug with water. Her daughter stood stunned.

"Wow! really, are you getting married?" she yells out with surprise and a pleased grin on her face.

"We've been to buy this engagement ring." She proudly stretched out her hand for Bridget to witness the sparkling diamond.

"Congratulation you two, she beamed, her voice penetrating the air with thrills of pleasure and hugs all round.

"We'll have a cuppa but won't stay long because you'll have things to do," she said to Bridget. "But I'm so happy that I had to come round." She beamed at her daughter.

"Oh that's really good mum, I'll text John (her husband) he'll be so pleased for you both."

They chatted about how big the diamond was and how it shone, giggling and discussing how she will fit a narrow width of gold wedding band later. Jonah sat quietly watching them twitter away without even attempting to get a word in. He just waited for the news to be digested. After a sit and a cup of tea, Gemma's excitement dissipates and all was calm again saying their goodbyes. She felt pleased that Bridget was happy for them, thank goodness.

Looking out of the passenger window they drove to Jonah's, relieved that her daughter's okay about her remarrying. All of the excitement had made her tired, it was the conclusion to a day of contrasts, where her mind had felt the disappointment followed by Bridget's over the moon reaction.

"Are you okay love?" he looked over at her.

"Yes, are you?" she enquired.

"It's the best thing that has ever happened to me, I love you so much," Jonah declared smiling.

"My ring is beautiful, I really love it, thank you, and it's not too ostentatious just very simple and lovely eh!"

"I knew you would choose something like that."

"Why?" she questioned him.

He laughed, "Money never impresses you, in fact you seem to avoid people knowing, and you never need to show it. That's one of the things I love about you."

"I suppose, it's nice to have wealth but I don't need it, I'm happy to live simply, but I do need you," she said with a shy smile.

"And that is exactly why you have me, and everything you'll ever need love." He reached over to give her hand a squeeze.

My goodness how could this momentous thing be happening to her? She wondered. Arriving back at Jonah's home she looked into his freezer to find something for tea.

Calling from the kitchen Gemma shouted loudly to Jonah, "You have fish cakes in here, shall we have them along with some peas and chips tonight, before I head off home to see Wilson."

"Sounds good love, I wish you were staying all night though," he said cautiously.

"I feel a need to go home; all the excitement has worn me out." A giggle escaped as she glanced down to admire the sparkles reflecting from her new jewellery.

"Go and get Wilson if you want, we can have an early night but I desperately want you to stay, we can have a spa when you get back and I'll get tea ready for you. He pleaded as he flips the spa pool lid open with a *bang* to check the temperature.

Pausing for a moment, to acknowledge the longing that she wanted to be with him as well.

"Okay," smiling back at him she flung her hands around his neck for a kiss, "I won't be long." Driving home with a newfound warmth settled inside, and a happy look of bliss, her face glowed with contentment. She tried not to worry about Violets negativity; she was sure the engagement was just something she would come to accept with time.

Wilson stood peering through the black gate that protected his bone from any roaming dogs. He watched and waited with a wagging tail for her to drive up to it. Opening the gate she gets greeted with a grand welcome.

"Stay down Wilson," Gemma's attempts to discipline him fail as he was too excited to heed anything. "Do you want to go for a ride to Jonah's house?"

He stopped in his tracks, that name worked magic as he calms to listen, "Okay, get in the car." Opening the back door for him to jump in before heading off to find a clean set of clothes for tomorrow morning, along with his dog food.

Jonah had delicious cooking smells wafting from the kitchen when she entered through the front door. The smell of fish crumbs toasting made her tummy growl, suddenly realizing she was hungry because they only had hot chocolate and cakes for lunch, while her ring was being resized.

The day had been lovely and emotionally exhausting all at the same time, and now the fatigue was impossible to ignore as she let Wilson into the orchard to run around, leaving the ranch slider open for him to return when he wanted.

"Let's eat, I'm starving." Gemma said.

"You're always hungry," he smiled while dishing fishcakes and vegetables.

They both laughed, he always teased her and the familiarity flooded her with warmth she enjoyed. After eating and relaxing in an armchair Wilson appeared for his tea, Gemma went to feed him outside before she undressed, ready to sink into the relaxing bubbling spa. Welcoming the hot water to help massage away the many emotions of the day.

Sitting side by side, they were not in there long enjoying the bubbles soothing powers when Jonah reached over to kiss her, after the height of excitement had today and with full stomachs now, the contentment and relaxation absorbed them both, along with an overwhelming need to get out of the water and go to bed, overcome with a burning desire he held her in his arms.

It had all been too much emotionally and after his warm kisses, and cuddles they lay in each other's arms and she slid into a light sleep, her mind starting to wander and dream, her breathing hastened as she visualized herself lying on the floor with hands tightening around her throat, gasping for air. Gemma was heated and frightened, waking with a jolt her horrified eyes only to find Jonah's hand lying peacefully on her chest. She was remembering the horrific assault when her ex-husband Mason attempted to strangle her. Sitting upright in bed Jonah was watching, deep in thought.

"Are you okay? I don't want to open old wounds but do you need to talk about it?" he asked sympathetically. A hairy paw suddenly flopped onto her arm and Wilson was there as well, watching.

"I'm okay little guy," she reassured him, giving his soft head a little pat, "Sometimes I find it hard to believe I'm still here, still alive. I know that I was lucky to have survived back then. I sometimes wonder how I managed to get up off the floor and run after being strangled, and I know it sounds weird, but I'm sure God helped me."

"Well, I'm not religious but I believe that when you're at deaths door amazing things can happen, it just hasn't happened for me because I've had no need of help I suppose. But if that was your experience, then I'm just glad he saved you to be with me." Jonah spoke with caring as he stood up to take Wilson to bed for her.

"I'll be fine, I think it's just that fear of my life changing again, away from the security of the cottage." Gemma said.

"The bible tells us.. *Isaiah 41:13 For I am the lord your God who takes hold of your right hand. Do not fear I will help you.*"

"It's still early enough to watch a movie on sky television if you want, I'll put the jug on?" suggested Jonah.

"Yes let's talk, why don't we have a cup of tea and talk about the wedding, how soon do you want to get married? Shall we leave it a while or have it soon?" Gemma queried as it was obviously unsettling her. Climbing out of bed and slipping on a cosy jumper before following him into the kitchen.

Jonah carried the two cups and they sat facing each other in the lounge. He began to express his concerns that they are not getting any younger and he would love to have her to wake up to every morning. Gemma sat watching the sincere look on his face and listened. This wonderful man melted her heart as he continued to show caring with his words.

"Let's live life to the full, we need to find a house we both love and one where I can put my boat into the water, I want to stop working and go fishing. We can travel and do whatever you like for the rest of our days, we never know how many we'll get. I'd like to get married as soon as you feel ready. What sort of wedding would you like?"

"Well, all I'm really concerned about is I want a traditional church wedding, an ivory coloured dress covered in feminine lace and a splattering of sequins with an oval neckline." She had already been thinking about it.

"It sounds like you need to find a good dress maker," he smiled, "You find one, I want you to have the best wedding ever, anything you want." He says.

"What do you want darling; you've never been married before." She pointed out.

"Church is okay, I don't want to wear any funny clothes though." He scrunched up his face.

"No, you don't need to wear long tails or anything, just a nice smart suit is what my prospective husband should be wearing, and I'd be happy if you could wear a royal blue tie with an ivory coloured shirt. I guess I can start looking and we can see what dates the church has available for us." She smiled and he looked ecstatic, like watching a satisfied bird soaring on just a breath of wind. "There's a lovely little inter-denominational church nearby so I'll make enquiries as to what dates they have available for our wedding."

After discussion with Jonah on how he felt about using the little heritage church and describing it to him with its off white walls and a matching white picket fence, they decided to go for a ride passed, and have a look to see if Jonah liked it. The fence was covered in thorny roses, and it had hydrangea bushes bunched along the inside of the fencing which were cut back to bare twigs at the moment. It must look lovely in summer. Having a look as they drove slowly passed they decided to stop and park out the front of the church and with it being closed, went for a walk around.

Gemma received a pleasant surprise as she walked on the brick pathway to the side of the church and followed around the corner to find a trellis archway. Standing with grandeur on the back lawn, surrounded by sheltering trees which would make another brilliant spot for photos. After discussion, it was decided that it must be a summer wedding with help from a florist to fill the lovely church with beautiful flowers, what type of flower was yet to be decided. She was very happy.

On Sunday they went along to a service, to meet everyone and for her to check out the lovely interior with its woodsy smells and solid old arched timber ceiling inside, the woodwork was amazing and she got a good feel for it. Mixing and meeting the parishioners was hospitable, she did a rough calculation in her head as to how many people they could seat in the pews. Following a lovely service, lots of smiles and goodbyes they headed off back to Jonah's to discuss if it suited them. The need was to now make a list of family and friends that they wanted to invite. Gemma's wedding list of things to do began, first she will phone the church on Tuesday and find out what dates they had available this coming summer. They have both decided to try and get around the 22$^{nd\,of}$ February 2021.

This mid-August winter weather was rather tiresome at the moment, and if February was possible it would give them a good six months to organize invitations, her dress and a reception venue in Auckland somewhere not too far from the church, which would be handy for everyone. Gemma was well aware that venues were always booked well ahead of a wedding, which brought a rush of nerves and butterflies to her stomach. Remedying that fear with thoughts of worst case scenario they could always have a marque in Jonah's paddock in summer, and with hiring and caterers Gemma would be happy with that. In fact, she believed it might be worth suggesting to Jonah that they should consider the idea.   With it being close to the house it would be more comfortable for her to change and relax, and guests might also enjoy it more than a venue hall.

Chapter 3

Looking online at different venues and mulling it over, her gut feeling was that she preferred the marque idea, thinking that she would find it difficult to tolerate being stuck inside for the reception, anxiety in that situation could ruin their day, so feeling concerned, she phoned up Jonah.

Jonah answered sounding worried, "Hello, what's wrong." He could see by the caller display that it was Gemma phoning.

"No, it's nothing, everything's fine. I've been looking for a venue for the wedding reception because I've heard back from the church and we can have the date we want to be married, the 22nd of February next year," she giggled with excitement. "But I couldn't wait to ask you if you would mind if we had the reception at yours instead, with a big marquee in the paddock next to the house? I know that being Auckland you can never trust the weather and we would have the house as a back up. A marquee would make a wonderful dramatic affect with lighting and stands of flowers; I think it would be lovely. I don't really want to feel shut into a large room with lots of people and the marquee opens up with a roof overhead to protect us from hot sun. What do you think?" She blurted out her concerns with her heart a flutter, her stomach feeling like a hundred excited butterflies all spreading their wings for the first time.

Any anxiety Gemma had felt was now gone; she was ready to make a commitment of marriage. She was looking forward, but there was still the possible fear of socializing after living a solitary lifestyle for so long. For now, one step at a time she felt an urgency to get everything organized, so the wedding would go off smoothly.

"Oh, I don't mind. I think you're right; it would look amazing situated in the paddock and would be convenient for us to use the house if we want. As long as you don't do anything, we'll need lots of helpers, caterers to deal with the food and a bar man to sort out drinks for everyone, with trays going around with canapes and all that." He said.

"Yes, I'll sort out lots of people to do the work, I know I can't get involved as it's our special day," she laughed at how well he knew her and she attempted to change the subject.

"Do you want to invite your mum and sister around this weekend for Sunday lunch and I'll cook a roast chicken?" She enquired; she really wanted them to like her.

"Yeah, that sounds like a good idea. I think they'll want to know all about the wedding plans." Jonah agreed.

"Okay, you sort that out and I'll go looking for the right sized marquee and check availability for our big day." Hanging up the phone as relief flooded over her, clearing her head and diminishing any anxiety of being closed in, it was agreed, no inside venue.

Reaching for her wedding folder, she has now made a good start. It was already bulging with information, samples and things to do. Shuffling through and grasping the invitation list in her hand, she began to count friends and family to invite and it totalled 62 people.

Gemma made a scribbled note, that they probably don't need a really big marquee. Excitement filled her once again as she set about searching online to see what was available, how thrilling as she had never looked at marquees before and what a wonderful surprise when she came across the perfect wedding frame marquee without any centre poles to get in the way, allowing for 75 people. That would give them extra spacing between rows of tables making for a formal seating arrangement but with room to move. They provide installation and removal for just under the $2,500 mark. After a quick gasp at the price she assured herself that Jonah wouldn't mind. It looks beautiful online and so much more intimate to have a marquee at home with its soft silk folds cascading down from the centre in white, plus they provide the tables, chairs and wedding arch at an extra cost. Gemma was convinced that Jonah would love it when she shows him the photos.

Jotting down, that she still needed to enlist experienced professionals to sort out the lighting and everything for them. She then sent some photos to her printer and would add them to the expanding folder to show Jonah, Violet and Pam when they come for lunch.

Gemma began to phone around for a good bridal shop to make the dresses, Bridget was thrilled to be her mum's maid of honour when Gemma asked her and wants to wear a royal blue dress in a flowing loose fit, the lace fabric lined and overlaid with a sprinkling of hand sewn sequins styled with a tight fitting boat neckline. Gemma made use of available online chatting to arrange an appointment with a bridal boutique for next week. The fabric, lace and style all needed to be agreed to and she wanted to explain exactly what she wanted so they could prepare the quote. She made the appointment for 3 pm so hopefully Bridget could come with her after she finished work. It would be useful for her to explain her ideas on style and fabric she would like, might as well get both dresses quoted together and have a lovely mother/daughter time as well.

Gemma was looking forward to it and was confident in the designer, even though she hadn't met Jean yet, she seemed to understand what was required over the phone. Jonah had insisted on paying for the dresses as well, even though Gemma felt that she should. He wouldn't hear of it. Jonah gleans pleasure from making her happy and she enjoys receiving so she accepts his ways. Thinking about it, she understood that to deprive him of enjoyment while being too independent would be wrong, he loved caring for her and she should let him. It was all such an emotional and sentimental journey! Gemma can not quite believe that it is not a fairy tale.

The wedding ceremony is for them both not just for her, with all the glamour, flowers and pretty wedding dress to wear. After Bridget and she explained to Jean(the dress maker) what is required then she will be able to say how long it will take to make the two dresses, quote how much it will cost and once that is all agreed to and fabrics sourced Gemma explained that it will be a summer wedding and request she not make the dresses until after winter, in case they change in size a little, what with the treats in front of the fire and cuddled up indoors all winter.

Gathering some examples of invitations and matching envelopes from the local printers she put them aside to show Jonah the colour, style and wording was still to be decided on. They planned to have each guests name printed on the invitation, she definitely did not want a run of the same and then her having to hand write the names on each one, her handwriting was not good enough.

The day disappeared while she spent more time perusing through designs for invitations and finding out how long it will take for printing, before tossing it all into her folder to take to show Jonah on Friday night when she stays over for the weekend. Jonah has said he'll ask his mate Mike to be his groomsman; he's a bit on the tall side with pale blue eyes and blonde hair and will look stunning in a grey suit and royal blue tie. It will be wonderful to have all their friends and family present at the wedding and she was exuberant to be marrying Jonah, even though summer still seems a long way off.

Turning into his driveway, rattle rattle from the car wheels carefully crossing over the cattle grid she drove towards the garage to park. She had packed an overnight bag and dog food ready to have a great weekend. Pausing for a second while she beeped the horn so Jonah would open the electric garage door, only a few seconds to wait before the door squeaks and shudders, causing Wilson to expectantly woof, he was hardly able to contain himself leaping around on the back seat as much as space allowed for a dog of his size. He was clever enough to know that when she parked in the garage, he got to stay for a few days and he loved that idea!

Wilson would have a chance to play with different dog toys and sometimes Jonah offered a surprise new toy to spoil him with. After gliding slowly into park she released the hound, he leapt out of the car and ran into the house, intent on finding Jonah as she reached for her tartan overnight bag from the passenger seat. She could hear laughter and thunderous big feet running through the house, Wilson had tracked down Jonah as they both burst forth through the open ranch slider.

"What about me?" Gemma light-heartedly howled out.

"Do you need a hand love?" came the query heard somewhere from up the hallway.

"No, I'm fine," she sighed wishfully as his arms reached out to pull her slim body closer, tucking her in close to his chest. Looking up and sinking into the depth of deep brown eyes she felt the warmth of his mouth on her lips for a brief moment before he moved away.

"I like Friday nights when I can stay over and get to cuddle you all night," she whispered affectionately.

"Not long now and you'll be here all the time, once we're married," he chuckled. "You'll be all mine."

"Yes. When you go fishing I'll go to the cottage to do gardening and visit the park and beach with Wilson, you know that eh!" she queried to reassure herself of her independence.

"Of course, and we can both spend the odd weekend there for a holiday at the beach if you want to. I've no intention of keeping you captive like in your last marriage." He looked on concerned that she was taking his joking seriously.

Jonah seemed to understand that in her past life she was duty bound to care for her sick husband 24/7, sometimes she wanders how she will cope if the urge to run away back to the beach continues and how she will manage after they marry.

"It'll be fine, you'll see, you enjoy the orchard and you can go to the cottage anytime you want, I'm fine with you being independent. Gradually you will learn to live with me and you'll find that this will become your home," he says confidently.

"Can I order new drapes for the lounge?" she teased.

"Anything you want, we'll go shopping together. I know your past husband was too sick to go into a shop so I understand a lot of things are strange for you." He held her in his arms and hugged, she felt stronger and more confident when together and she nodded in agreement.

"Are your mum and sister coming on Sunday?"

"Yes, Pam will bring her. They didn't know what time so I have to text that to Pam."

"Let's eat about 1 o'clock eh? But they can come before that if they want."

"I'll send a message tomorrow, let's spend tonight together without any interruptions, he reached for another hug, pulling her closely into his body, their lips touched and what was only going to be a quick kiss soon turned into something very different, she pulls away giggling self-consciously.

"Hey, do you want to put the dog food in the fridge and I'll take my bag to the bedroom," she suggested as she started to unwind from the comfort of his arms and the desirable aroma of musky after shave permeating her nostrils.

"Okay, no rush to be close to you we have the whole weekend," he interjects.

"Of course darling, is it cheese on toast and then a spa tonight?" She was thinking out loud.

"Sounds good to me, I'll get the wine for us, do I need to feed Wilson for you?" he offered.

"Not yet thanks, he just wants to run in the orchard for a while, then when we have ours, I'll feed him."

Flopping down on the bed she removed her shoes, trousers and pulled on one of his big shirts that he had thrown over the armchair, it's a generous size to cover his muscular shoulders and she felt comfortable wrapped in him, smelling of his musky scent before going into the kitchen to prepare toasted cheese, only to find Jonah was already slicing the cheese for her. Carefully arranged under the grill she called Wilson to come in and get his tea.

Any mention of food and he appears instantly like magic, they both laughed at how smart he was. Setting his food on the ground and putting theirs on the outdoor table Gemma sat, 'bang' Jonah opened the lid of the spa and steam billowed up.

"Awe that looks inviting, I've felt the cold biting today."

After relaxing and finishing up in the kitchen they strip off, taking the wine over to the side of the pool before climbing in. Lounging in the bubbles Jonah gazed deeply into her eyes while he ran his finger down her shoulder, shivers ran down her skin enticing her to move in closer, the course skin of a farmers hands against her own smooth bare shoulder combined with the warm water to create a hot over-whelming sensation. She was mindful of the intimate closeness of their naked bodies; she was determined to distract them both onto something else.

"The red folder I dumped on the coffee table is full of wedding information," she explained. "We can look at it tomorrow and get a bit more sorted before we see your mum and sister on Sunday."

Averting her eyes away from his gorgeous masculine naked upper body jutting out of the bubbling water.

"Are you happy with how it's coming together so far?" he asked.

"Yes, it's all falling into place really well, it's been very easy to sort out, and Bridget and I are booked in to see the dressmaker at 'Brides Sorted' next week. Hopefully, if that all goes well we'll know what we are wearing." Her bright smile showing how happy she was.

The penetrating warmth of the bubbly water frothed and sizzled around her cold frame, easing away any muscle tension, along with the bubbles in the wine making her lightheaded, relaxed and demanding total attention. Everything else could wait, Gemma was aware of how much she wanted to be in bed with him.

Waking up to brightness lighting up the drapes Saturday morning, she found her arm was draped across his waist.

They had slept in, fulfilled with a happy warmth comfortably settled within her, it was nothing like a physical thing, this connection ran far deeper.

Breathing in slowly he still smelt of soap from the shower he had before climbing into bed last night, Gemma's head nestled in the space on top of his shoulder next to his ear, every nerve ending alive with feeling, just to be beside him in the morning set her on fire. She was sexually excited so slid down the bed to reach his mouth, he stirred and opened his eyes just as her lips reached his and her heartbeat faster as their tongues entwined. He whispered good morning in a seductive sound, precipitating heavy breathing and lying on top of his outstretched body he remained still allowing her to explore him. Running a warm hand down his chest, she discovered him. He was average build but wrestling with calves and hay bales had done amazing things to his upper strength.

His waist narrow with strong thighs, and as she stopped looking she went for another passionate warm kiss, wet and arousing. Her whole body tucked down in his arms. Not speaking, they just lay there breathing in the moment.

Jonah spoke, "I'm glad we are happy together, would you like breakfast?" he asked her, gently stroking her hair.

"Yes please I'm hungry."

"You're always hungry."

Both laughing he started to climb out of bed to spend Saturday together. Wilson had been very good sleeping in a little longer this morning, but he could be heard shuffling in the spare bathroom. Gemma went to let him out, to what looked to be a beautiful clear day. The water pump purred into action when Jonah turned on the tap to fill the electric jug.

Serenity, it was blissfully quiet as they sat at the outdoor table enjoying breakfast together, the quietness was peace enhancing. They watched as Wilson sniffed around the fence line, Jonah pipped up with an important announcement.

"I'm glad we're getting married soon, because not being allowed to be with you completely is killing me!"

Gemma laughed, "As long as we're close and can talk about sex you'll survive." Sex outside of marriage had always seemed an unnecessary experiment to her. Urgent moments of wonderful desire could be so easily dampened later by guilt.

"It's hard to wait, but I'm worth it," she told him.

"No wonder I have more grey hair since I met you," he laughed as well.

"Complexities of life are never easy but good things come to those who wait. Let's have a look for berries in the orchard." Pushing her chair back and rising to wander around.

Jonah had not yet finished his coffee, so firmly gripping the mug handle he pushed himself up off the chair, ready to carry it with him as they walk. They investigate and chat about all the lovely lime green growth shooting out from the citrus trees. Life in a garden always filled her soul with joy; to watch the miracle of new life springing forth and old branches or plants dying back from disease, damage and poor nutrition as they struggle to thrive, this was life, to be celebrated was to show our appreciation of that.

They found a few fruit to eat and then leaving Wilson to run around they continued out of the fenced orchard, and across the wet paddock wearing stylish red band gumboots to look over the cattle and deer. Huge pine trees lined the metal race as they continue on walking through puddles and muddy ground where the animals had clustered together in expectation of going through the next gate. Jonah assured her that no animals were loose in the race and it was quite safe outside the electric fencing.

He turned to her and stopped walking, with a serious face he began to speak his mind, "While you make plans for our wedding I'm going to put 100 hectares on the market to sell and I want to start looking for our home, somewhere to moor the boat. What do you think?"

Compassionately she hesitates with her reply, "Yes, we can do that in our spare time." She was uneasy, parting with his lifestyle would be a major move for him to contemplate.

Jonah began to explain, that although he had sometimes looked to move in the past, circumstances have changed now that he is getting married, he wants to include her and so they both have to agree on where and what type of home to live in.

"That's lovely darling, as long as it's not too far out of Auckland as I still want to enjoy my cottage garden until I get another garden established elsewhere."

"I'm hoping that we will find you a beautiful new garden and you can personalize that to your hearts content while I go fishing," he smiled and gently squeezed her hand.

"So our wish list is near Auckland, mooring for your boat, relaxing outdoor area, room for the dog to run around and if the kitchen is no good I'll need a new one installed." Gemma explained light-heartedly.

"That's about it, but it must also be level, definitely no steps as we get older, internal garage entry for at least two cars, we can always have a boat carport put up somewhere. An easy to maintain place that we can grow old together, no more livestock for me," he said.

"Yes no more work, just play." She stretched out her arms to reach around his neck and they enjoyed a long seductive tongue twisting happy kiss before she pulled away letting out a shy giggle.

They had strolled a long way from the house, so holding hands quietly started to walk back. Gemma's mind was full of private thoughts and dreams.

Chapter 4

All of his animals looked healthy and well fed, Jonah pointed out the paddock holding thirty incredibly huge cattle ready to go to the meat works, and it was amazing how the paddocks appeared immaculately groomed, the animal's tongues rap around every long blade of grass before munching through it. A lot of the paddocks were empty of animals, still closed off, to allow for fresh lush food to grow for later. Still hand in hand, they stood looking out over undulating land, separated into large paddocks with strong posts, wire and electrical fencing bordered by established pine trees that provided shade and wind breaks for the vigorous animals. Gemma found it awesome to see how people and nature can work together to produce food without damaging the beautiful environment.

Wedding arrangements were well underway, the church and the marquee were booked and she will also hire the quantity of tables and chairs from the same company closer to time, once the numbers were established. Gemma decided to purchase white tablecloths and had made a note in the folder to buy royal blue ribbon to wrap around the chair backs, she plans to create large decorative bows, also adding a note to check with the florist what flowers will be available for 22nd February.

Gemma was reasonably sure of getting the roses which are grown year round and has been advised that the white sweet peas might need to be especially grown, the florist was checking on that for her.

Arriving back at the house, they slip out of muddied gumboots after entering the airy laundry area and walk through to the beautiful cream coloured lounge, content to sink into a comfy armchair to relax for five minutes after a demanding walk back up the sloping race.

It didn't take long before Jonah revived, heartened by their future plans together he felt strengthened and excited that life was so good.

"Let's put on some music," he says. "Now the folder is sorted out put it away and dance with me." Leaping out of his chair and stretching out his hand for her to take, he gave a small tug to pull her to standing and hugged her tight.

"Okay darling, do you have any bubbles to drink?"

"Coming right up my love!" Heading to the kitchen, to pour two crystal glasses of Sauvignon Blanc.

Gemma set up the music. What a wonderful afternoon just the two of them, Wilson had been left running in the orchard away from the cattle to keep him safe and he came bounding into the kitchen. He then ran off outside to retrieve a biscuit thrown onto the lawn while Gemma pulled the ranch slider closed, preventing him getting in the way and disrupting the dance moves. Wilson was so lovable and tried to get included in everything Gemma did.

While bending over to look at the CD's that are tidily stored in the vertical slots of a black plastic stand, her short skirt rode up just enough to reveal the lace edging around the legs of a pair of skimpy lace bikini knickers, just as he returned. She looked up to see him bringing in the drinks and asked if he had a favourite tune, his starry eyes gave him away, the poor fellow obviously yearned for something other than a dance.

"You are my favourite, but I must settle for an Elvis CD I suppose." He responded kindly.

Ignoring his comment, she cheerfully responded. "Here it is, let's do Rock n Roll followed by some slow ballroom." Smiling before quickly turning back to the CD collection, she tried diversion.

Putting the two wine flutes on the coffee table Jonah then sauntered across the room toward her, reaching out he gently pulled her into his arms, facing each other. Gemma's eyes watering as she looked deeply into the abyss of dark brown, sending hot shivers through her stomach area. A tender kiss and he started to sway, with her held securely in his arms his lips firmly pressed on hers. She slowly breathed in his sweet smell, an interesting mix of soap and perspiration remaining from the walk. He proceeded to turn her hand gently downwards to be in the correct dance position, implying that he was trying to focus on dancing, both harbouring a hunger for passion.

The faster the music, the more boisterous their spinning and focus on the music, they tuned their minds and bodies to go full on into all of the Rock n Roll routines. It was fun and any erotic sensations or ideas held were swished away. They laughed and improved on the more difficult lifts and twists; Elvis came to an end and they both collapsed exhausted onto the sofa for a well-deserved drink.

"Wow that was fast, we did really well eh?" she said glowing up at him.

"We did. I think we dance well together; do you need your drink filled up again?" he asked.

"Just a little more then," she laughed, after all that exercise another one won't hurt."

After a few more sips of wine while relaxing on the sofa his arm went around her shoulders and the kissing became more intense, long wet kisses as his tongue searched hers and waves of electricity surged through her once again. After several gulps of Sauvignon Blanc her will power dwindled and she ended up lying down. Spread out on the sofa as the cushions were thrown to the floor, he lay beside her pulling up the edge of her skirt.

"No," she whispered to him.

"I won't, I just want to touch and look at you, kissing gently and the air alive with hastened breathing and rapid heartbeats, it was a beautiful moment of closeness. Jonah was not acting out of lust, but love and caring, she was with him as her hands also explored. The trust they had in each other was very special, he was attractive and also considerate of Gemma's feelings, those things combining to send contented shivers running around her entire body, for a magical moment they lay entwined in each other's arms, a spiritual awareness and physical presence. She was ready to trust her life to this man in marriage, his love was a risk worth taking.

Sunday morning, she prepared the roast with slivers of garlic carefully pushed under the chicken's skin before putting it back into the fridge for a while, ready for lunch later.

"Jonah, what time are your mum and sister coming do you know?" she calls out from the kitchen.

"They decided that to prevent mum getting tired they would come about 12.00pm and only stay until after lunch. That will give them time to chat about the wedding arrangements while lunch is cooking." Jonah called from the dining room while he flicked open a crisp ecru coloured tablecloth, it accurately spread across the wooden table.

"Do you think your mum is worried that she might not see you very often when you get married?"

"I don't know, she's old and I've never been married, so I suppose it's a new idea for her to take in."

"Hmm." Gemma wondered.

They both get busy peeling vegetables and Gemma made an apple sponge pudding for afterwards, leaving it on the bench covered with a tea-towel for later. When Violet and Pam arrived they sat down with cups of tea and hot coffee, Gemma didn't need to be in the kitchen now that the roast was in the oven cooking. Delicious cooking smells drifted in the air and ignited their taste buds as they sat reading and discussing wedding arrangements.

Pam congratulated them with a genuine smile, "You are just what my brother needs," she says. "It's about time, he's not getting any younger."

"Thanks." Gemma replied as relief flooded over her. One down and one to go she thought.

They were sitting in the lounge like strangers, Gemma careful not to upset her future relatives, the tension was thick in the air and she was appreciative of Pam's support, taking a stand for her brothers happiness. Violet only spoke when she couldn't help herself, curiosity getting the better of her, as she inquired about something to do with the wedding plans. She never looked Gemma's way, only addressed Jonah or looked out of the window. Gemma refused to let it worry her, Violet was old and she and Jonah were getting married, full stop!

Lunch was faultless. Jonah offered to get it out of the oven, carefully carrying the heavy oven dish full of lovely golden roast vegetables and crispy skinned chicken to put on the breadboard for carving. It looked and smelt wonderful with everything cooked to perfection. He then piled the platter high with vegetables while Gemma made the gravy on the stove top, as it simmered she continually stirred, not allowing it to go lumpy. Two beautiful matching platters, one with assorted vegetables the other with carved chicken were taken to the table. Jonah also took over the tureen of carrots and peas she had ready, while she calmly carried the white porcelain gravy boat to the table before returning to the kitchen to put the apple pudding in to cook.

Pleasantries were exchanged, the usual weather conversations and what everyone had been up to. Jonah continued to pour wine as needed. After enjoying the pudding and cream, Violet let out a huge sigh and it wasn't long before they left for home. Gemma was satisfied that she had done her best and that's all anyone could do.

She and Jonah sat quietly, the lunch had gone okey, although they had both felt the distance and coolness from Violet, neither of them mentioned it, didn't want to confront it. This was their upcoming marriage and they didn't want any negativity, only wanting for everyone to share in the happiness they had for each other.

Jonah walked up to her, taking her in his arms, "Thank you for a wonderful family lunch love." He said.

"That's okey, I'm glad it was nice and they get to be involved in our arrangements. They didn't really have any suggestions, although Pam said she thought having a marquee was a great idea," she smiled.

"Yes, it will suit me better than in a church." He wandered off to the kitchen, Gemma could hear him adding water to the jug as the water pump kicked in.

They both sat silently nursing a cup of tea, relaxing after saying goodbye to his mum and sister, the tension was still lingering for Gemma and the powerful desire for her to run back home was challenging to ignore. At the same time she sympathised with Jonah and how he must be feeling as he was in the middle of it.

"Well, I suppose I better go home soon and let you have some peace and quiet," she said awkwardly.

Their eyes met as he looked sorrowfully from across the room. She gulped the last of her tea down quickly, taking the cup to the sink before going to pack her week-end bag and gather Wilson's things ready to go home. Everything was quickly flung into the boot of the car, her mind and emotions in scrambled confusion and she was a little upset, Jonah came over to her.

"I'd like to take you up north next Saturday to show you the land I want to sell," he said.

"Oh, isn't it part of this land here? I just imagined it was."

"No, I have more land further out on the way to Waterworth so do you want to have a look next weekend?" he asked as he stood in front of her and held her lightly by the elbows.

"Yes, I'd love that."

"Great, we'll buy some lunch out and make a day of it." The family was forgotten and a smile spread across his face, the tension eased as they shared a quick kiss goodbye before she headed off.

Driving home with Wilson in the safety and familiarity of the car she was relieved that the lunch was over and contemplated on the strange silence that ensued after his family had left. Perhaps Jonah was worried that Gemma was upset, or perhaps he also noticed the deplorable way his mother never acknowledged Gemma, directing all her queries about the wedding plans to him. It could have been a more pleasant lunch, and it might be something Jonah has to get used to, if he doesn't say something to his mum. Gemma was just glad to see the look of relief on Jonah's face, he knew she would not let anyone deter her. She still wanted to go out with him next weekend.

Back home, the first thing to do was go down to the beach with her devoted little dog, he had been so good playing outside in the orchard during lunch at Jonah's. Breathing in the crisp sea air and viewing the beach that had been never ending and predictable, always there for her during the last three years, she had been the one to change and grow. Endlessly amazed by the sun, sea and wildness of nature was refreshing in mind and body and she had a new freshness to life. A hopeful future to be shared with an amazing man.

"Thank you Lord for leading me to this wondrous place to heal."

Friends frequently asked her how she found such a quiet place, because it was so out of the way and off the beaten track. Pondering for a moment, she had to admit she couldn't remember how. For some strange reason long ago she remembers telling agents and friends she wanted to buy a place at Latent Beach.

Gemma believed it was God's plan she was unaware of; he wanted her to move there. Like a lost forgotten place that wouldn't suit everyone, but it was very special to her. Sitting at the favourite park bench Wilson lay at her feet, he seemed content to be home too.

The weather was changing and the wind roughened the waves, swishing up slimy brown seaweed, the appearance being a great deterrent not to touch it, along with the putrid smell of sulphide gas that was being emitted after hours of it laying on the sand.

Instead of the expected salty smell it was now reminiscent of rotten eggs. However, the shrill sound of the seagulls cries brought back fond memories of her childhood along with the splash of the jumping fish as they flop back into the water. It was pleasant and relaxing as they ambled their way up to the reserve, at peace and stress free again, this place would be very difficult to leave.

Walking along the sea wall watching the tide sweeping in, it swished up against the sandstone and splashes landed on her beach shoes like a greeting. A brief hint of sadness and questioning suddenly pressed on her mind as she wondered if she would survive not living there anymore but reassuring herself Jonah was happy to spend some weekends at the cottage. All is not lost, and maybe absence will make the heart grow fonder and when she returns she will be even more appreciative of the beach, and the significance it played instructing her of her diminutive part in this immense universe.

Wilson and Gemma continued to walk and sometimes ran in the foaming edge of the sea for the rest of the week, and as it drew to an end Friday night she again drove to Jonah's place, to stay for the weekend.

"Hi, it's just us," calling out, they arrive to find the front door left open.

She headed for the bedroom to dump her bag down in the corner of the room, before going through the ranch slider that was also open. Wilson bounded up to Jonah who he found fossicking in the orchard doing this and that. It was good that Jonah enjoyed growing the fruit trees and finding the hidden berries quite rewarding. Smiling, he tilted the bowl to show her it was half full of boysenberries, a contented smile spread on his face.

"How are you love?" he asked as he reaches to plant a little peck on her check.

"I'm good, looking forward to going out for a ride tomorrow." She gave a short friendly rub on his back.

"Yes, we can have a sleep in though, as it will only take about an hour to get there, it's around 50 Km away."

Gemma spent time wandering amount the trees and they enjoyed chatting about how well everything was growing, while they checked the stakes were still securely in the ground with Wilson running around. They added a few more ties on any new growth that could potentially be snapped off by wind. Jonah found a few raspberries then carefully handed then to her to eat. They felt comfortable together, her face flushed with a joyful glow.

Gemma decided to make the pizza tonight, she knew Jonah always had a good supply of cheese so she had brought an onion, tomato relish to slather on the base, plus spicy hot salami sausage, and the green capsicum she likes. Fetching a bowl out of the cupboard she set about making the pizza base which she did all the time for herself at home, she never bought ready made pizza.

Jonah stood watching, his face considering, thoughtful and kind, he quietly asked, "Would you like a coffee or can I help grate the cheese for you?"

"Yes please, grate the cheese, I don't like doing that in case I grate my long nails," she laughed.

Unafraid and finding it fun to have him in the kitchen while she cooked. It was unusual for her; she was always hesitant to have someone that close. Deep in thought she realized her life had changed, she had evolved from a cocoon, was more trusting and was becoming like an exploring butterfly. Well, with Jonah anyway.

They sipped on wine and the side salad went untouched, the pizza emitted inviting aromas, and although Wilson was having a run around in the orchard the smell soon brought him inside, he reappeared at the ranch slider. Gemma headed off to feed him while Jonah cleared the table and they decided to finish the balmy evening relaxing in the therapeutic hot spa pool. The cool refreshing air lightly blew away another week of being apart.

Chapter 5

Settling down for the night she was surprised when she woke from a sound sleep, her head had hit the pillow, and it was already morning like she had only just laid down. Gemma was beginning to feel very comfortable sleeping with Jonah, as if it were meant to be.

Wilson trailed her outside his nose high up in the air, as she carried a gigantic bone hoping to keep him busy all day, placing it on the ground she then went to fill her drinking bottle with water, laying it in the car ready to head off to view Jonah's property. During the drive Jonah suggested a nice bakery where he loved to buy his favourite home baked apricot pies and salad sandwiches. They made that the first stop, purchasing some goodies to take for later on when they got peckish.

It was a pleasant drive until they entered the dusty loose metaled road and pulled onto Jonah's property. First glance rendered her speechless, it took her breathe away with it's beautiful established native trees, where Manuka and huge Totara had been allowed to spring up naturally. She pointed at a natural waterfall running down from the hills, meandering around and creating a cool clear pond, before coming to rest in a hollow at the bottom where some trenching had been done. Taking the overflow water along through each paddock with a network of black polyethylene pipes that filled each water trough for the few animals he left there.

He explained how it worked, with the pump housing in a small shed at the far end of the property, hidden behind a massive mature pine forest that was nearing the end of its life, soon to be felled and milled for timber. Standing in the morning sun on the edge of the rise, a clear blue sky and rolling meadows everywhere. Gemma looked out over the breath taking view, her disbelieving eyes began to fill with tears, it was ridiculous to feel so overwhelmed, but she choked up in awe, it was all so beautiful. Embarrassed, she had to turn away so Jonah didn't see how emotional she was.

It had been a mild winter so they were able to drive though several gates before leaving the four wheeled vehicle behind, as they trudged uphill on foot the rest of the way. They walked and pushed a track in through a paddock of waist high grass to get to the top of the hill, she was hot and exhausted. Walking in the wide open spaces where the scorching sun blazed down on their heads was also challenging.

Jonah explained that when he was on his own he used a small farm bike, eventually they fought their way to the highest point and looked out in awe over the magnificent vista, Gemma wiped her glistening face on the bottom of her shirt as they smiled at their achievement. Certain that they had earnt a sit and rest up against a cliff for some shade. Jonah reached in to retrieve lunch from the backpack he thankfully removed from his shoulder; he laid it on the ground. Looking out over expansive green open spaces with rolling hills and huge native trees scattered between meadows again brought tears to her eyes, she promptly wiped them away feeling rather silly, that she could be reduced to tears just being in this wilderness, it was so beautiful. Gemma pondered about the many farms now gone, cut up into small plots over the years, and they now hold multi story town houses, with few parking spaces for all the city dwellers who crowd into what was once, green countryside like this.

Being confronted with this magnificent sight she anguished over the shame that we populate everywhere to overflowing, how can civilization sustain this growth, losing all the wide open spaces with people living longer and increasing the need for more schools and childcare facilities so mothers can go to work. People have changed so much in this modern world of ours, from being content to go without a telephone, to now, even children carry a mobile. As she sat contemplating life, she remembered first getting married, they went without furniture and a television to be able to afford the mortgage on their first home.

"Are you sure you want to sell this?" she gasped while wiping the tears away. "I can't believe you really own it."

No words could express the unexplained pleasure she derived from this natural beauty, overwhelming her. "I've never seen anything like this, except in movies. It's a shame to sell it off, what will happen to it?" she pleaded for an answer.

"It has council approval to be cut up into one hectare lots, but I'm thinking of protecting it with a covenant, so it must be five hectare lots. That means the houses will be scattered around leaving it greener and more attractive, making small lifestyle blocks people can still have a few animals or grow food. I'll get my planner to work out if I can sell only 20 lots and how I can fence and get power to each one before selling them." He explained.

Linking her arm around his, Gemma's voice breaks as she struggled to hold back tears of joy, "Oh yes, do that," she paused before speaking. "It feels very spiritual here."

The hushed, humble drive home went quickly as they pulled into the garage. Gemma couldn't wait to cuddle Wilson who was his usual excited self and greeted them with full body wagging, he was so pleased to see them.

Jonah's suggestion that they climb into the spa to unwind and relax tired muscles was a welcome idea. They both dropped their dusty clothes onto the bedroom floor and stepped naked into the soothing warm water as Gemma collected her thoughts. Jonah began to explain how he picked up the land very cheaply many many years ago because it was so far out, away from where anyone would want to live. Now the city boundaries have moved out and it has grown into this wonderful place full of native flora and natural waterways.

Jonah's eyes met hers and she looked deeply into them, with a heartfelt thanks she expressed how amazing and special it was that he showed it to her. Stepping out of the heated water after a short time as she didn't want to become too relaxed and sluggish, pulling on a warm jumper and jeans she prepared to go home. Wilson followed as she put her belongings into the back of the car. Gemma opened the back passenger door and he straight away leapt into the back seat ready to return home; it had been an emotional day seeing that land and getting her head around the fact that one person could own such an incredible place.

Waking up warm and cosy in her own home Gemma scanned the bedroom, decorated in grey painted walls and pretty floral accessories, a modest size and nothing like Jonah's luxurious home with its tall glass doors and huge rooms, and from his bed he looks out onto lush paddocks, in contrast to her opening the delicate heritage lace curtains that look out onto a white picket fenced cottage garden with its private back yard, tree lined boundaries swaying in a gentle breeze, a sturdy black park bench tucked into the corner among multitudes of flowers from daisies, tall foxgloves, tiny low growing pansy which were companion to purple and white alyssum, nodding heads of old fashioned granny's bonnets and stately spires of hollyhocks in among multi coloured clumps of alstroemeria and scented carnations, how idyllic, romantic, and so appropriate for a lady to enjoy. The cobbled stone pathways she had pain stakingly laid herself weaving a way through the flora.

Looking with admiration at the creation viewed from on top of her lace edged duvet, her much loved cottage garden, sometimes she wavered in her thoughts but determined to move on, of course Jonah's home would be different, he said he wanted them to find something with a garden. With a bigger property and more space she will be able to make it even more spectacular! Gemma was sure that once God shows her the way all doubts would be gone and she would fall in love with their new home, together as they were meant to be.

It was difficult to imagine leaving this place of solace as she stood up to look out over her garden. Quickly shaking herself out of it she dressed cognizant of cooling temperatures, pulled on her jeans and long sleeve jersey knit top. She tied her hair into a coil and a clasp, a semblance of tidy if she ignored the wispy unruly bits insistent on escaping before she headed to give Wilson his breakfast.

While Wilson was happy having a run outside, the toaster pops up and she spread one slice with butter and marmalade before reaching for a hot mug of tea to have out in the garden. He ran up to her with a purple ball in his mouth assuming that she would play with him.

"I'm not playing, I'm having breakfast," amused she smiles down at him.

He dropped the ball and ran off to sniff out under the many trees. The day had started and after breakfast he received plenty of attention although she decided to forego a walk today, washed some windows, she knew the day and her energy always disappeared too quickly. Seven o'clock came around and Gemma's usual evening phone call eventuated once more.

"Hi, darling," Gemma chirped cheerfully down the phone.

"Hi, have you had a good day?" he asked.

"Yes, nothing special just a bit of housework and I baked some lemon tarts to use up some of the lemons on my tree. How about you, what did you get up to?" she enquired.

"I've sold a truck and trailer load of cattle today. That one I didn't trust refused to go up the chute and broke a fence railing, so the driver had to use the electric prodder. We got there in the end, so I think we should have a look for our new home on Saturday, what do you think."

"Oh really?" that came as a surprise.

"Yes, the real-estate agent I use all the time, has found a few houses for us to look at and they have open homes on them this Saturday. I've told her what we want and requested she keep an eye out. Would it be okay for you to have a look on Saturday?"

"Can do, where are they?" she enquired with simmering curiosity.

"One in Mahurangi and a couple up Waterworth way."

"That sounds okay, as long as they back onto water for your boat and have privacy."

"Oh yes, I told her not to bother me if it didn't have what we want, because we both have a home to live in there's no rush. Even if we get married next February you can move in here while we keep looking."

"That's right, would it take long to sell your home if we want to move."

"Shouldn't do, people will want the land, and I still have the holding up North we saw last Saturday. I really want to develop that before selling them off though."

"I'll see you Saturday morning, then we can head off. What time do you want to go?" she queried.

"Just as early as you can get here, bring Wilson he can stay over. Will you feel like going out Saturday night or not after our day of looking?" He asked.

"No, let's stay in and talk about what we find, that way we can spend time looking around the bays up Waterworth way before we come home, if the suns out we can make a day of it."

"See you Saturday, I'll ring you tomorrow night," he said.

"Okay, bye darling."

The week flew by, what with spraying edges while the weather held out and cutting everything back with the few imminent winter days too cold to be outside. Friday evening was welcomed with weary bones, and she looked forward to what Saturday may bring as she snuggled blissfully in between winter sheets, shuffling cold feet around and mindful that Jonah liked cotton sheets all year round. That will be a major change for her to get used to, she will need to get an electric blanket which she never had to do before. A clear Saturday morning breaks forth, albeit a bit cool. Jonah was ready to leave as her car pulled into his driveway.

"I've made a thermos of tea for me; I know you like your tins of fizz in the car as we drive around. I've packed some mandarins and potato chips to snack on the way, before having lunch," Gemma smiled confidently.

"Good idea love, are we ready to go?"

"Yes, I'll just put Wilson outside with his toys." She settled into Jonah's car and they headed off.

Gemma arranged the real estate photos and directions of the houses for sale, positioned on her knee ready to provide directions.

"This one looks nice. Shall we see the Mahurangi one first on our way, or go to the end and work back?"

After a thought they decide to see them in order as they come while driving and then drive straight back home after if they get tired or sick of looking.

Pulling into the first open home, it is well underway with two other couples looking through, they wander around outside and down to the water's edge, checking out the boat ramp and jetty area. Jonah thought it needed a lot of work as he pointed out dubious amounts of rotting timber. She was disappointed that there was no real garden, just boggy lawn which in parts they sloshed around in their shoes, it was obviously waterlogged and some parts were very steep to mow, without any real possibility for good growing soil and sun.

Large trees were shading everywhere, they noted that removing them meant exposing the property to neighbours and loosing privacy, plus it would be windy. The house was obviously someone's holiday home, not maintained and everything was old and dated. It needed a new kitchen, bathroom, painting and the concrete path running around the house was broken and non-existent in places.

Getting back into the car disillusioned, they struggled to find anything positive to say about it. Both agreeing that they would want to demolish and start again and hoped the next one was more to their liking. Traveling past Mahurangi and heading towards Waterworth

Gemma's blue eyes glued to the map, searching the streets to find the second house to view, pulling up outside they looked at it and then at each other, the house in question was sandwiched between neighbouring homes that were very close.

"Let's not bother to see this one, I couldn't stand hearing what's going on next door all the time," she said to Jonah quite assertively.

"I agree, where is the next one?"

"Looking at the agent's directions, I think it's just a few streets ahead of us."

Shuffling papers and photos around on her knee to find directions. Driving around the water's edge they find Amber Place, the last house on the list, pulling up outside No.8 which is her favourite number they face a ground level brick home.

Peering through the wooden gateway, "It looks like there's plenty of room to drive in," Gemma says.

"Okay, let's see." Jonah turns the car into the entrance way, up a wide sealed driveway ample for a boat trailer to travel, liquidambar trees staggered along the way with grass underneath. Gemma's mind was already visualizing what she would plant. Looking around and thinking that she would have daffodils and multiple spring bulbs planted in the lawn to make a brilliant spring display as you drive up to a dark brown brick, not a modern home, but a character home with colonial windows and French doors. Noticing its tall, steep roof in dark brown tiles. They circle around a central garden in the driveway nearing the house, containing a single aristocratic Magnolia taking centre stage, with brick edging around an otherwise empty garden.

"Wow! This is nice, I love the grounds, and it has real potential," Gemma cried out to Jonah almost jumping out of her seat to go and see more of this very promising home.

"Yes, at least the entrance is impressive, let's hope the rest is," he says cautiously interested.

A real estate agent appears from nowhere to greet them before they reach the front door, introducing herself as Penelope.

Her long blonde hair cascading down the back of a smart navy jacket and skirt, with practical slip-on and off shoes.

"Did you find the address okay?" she enquires politely. Gemma is excited to ask, "Yes thanks, how old is the house?"

"It's about thirty years old and the owners had it built in this style to reflect a different era; they still live here it has never been sold before. They are both getting on in years and have resolved that a retirement village is probably the best plan for them at this time in their lives. Feel free to wander around and ask me any questions while I see to the other couple that are already inside." Smiling she's suddenly gone as quickly as she appeared with a quick wave with her hand leaving them to look around.

"I'm impressed so far, aren't you. Let's look around outside while they're inside and then go in later," Gemma whispered as she pulled on Jonah's arm eagerly. Making a move to proceed around the grounds.

"I wonder how much garaging there is." Jonah thinks out loud.

Following the path around the side of the house with groups of shrubbery, they stop and stand in awe suddenly confronted with a three car garage, plenty of sealed area and a path continuing down one side of the section to the water's edge, they could already see a floating jetty bobbing up and down with the tide, making it easy to get on and off a boat. A broad smile swept across Jonah's face.

"Oh, this is good," he says smiling, disbelieving and excited.

"This is neat eh. I'm dying to see inside." Walking back to the house, they encounter a grass path bordered by giant balls of fading purple and blue Hydrangeas, now finished for the season on either side of it. They mosey down the path for a look.

"Oh look!" Gemma screeched loudly while squeezing his arm, unable to hold back a massive smile. "Oh, I can't believe this, it's stunning."

The grass path weaved around and they found themselves confronted with a small orchard with rows of established fruit trees.

"We better have a look inside before someone makes an offer," he whispers to her. "A property like this is rare to find."

The expansive solid wooden French doors are dark with gleaming brass handles opening into a large entranceway where dark iron, animal shaped coat hooks welcome you to hang outdoor attire. Walking though she was approving of the soft cream walls with sparkling tiles on the floor, before stepping onto the softness of thick pile carpet in the lounge. It lends an air of sophistication and has obviously been loved. The kitchen is a good size with an eyelevel oven and ample storage, with a long white marble slab breakfast bar or buffet, it was a sensational large bench space. Everywhere had sufficient light with tall glass doors opening to the outside from the lounge and dining, three bedrooms with floor to ceiling windows and beautiful drapes throughout the home.

"Oh Jonah this will cost a fortune to buy." She warned him, reluctant to fall in love with something she will never have.

"If it ticks all our boxes and we both love it then we'll make an offer, let's talk with the agent.

"Penelope," Jonah beckons to her, and she eagerly strides across the room to speak with them.

"How can I help?" she asks.

"We are interested in making an offer, we're going outside to talk about it, and I'll phone you soon okay." He explained.

"I'll be here." She smiled warmly.

Heading for the car to sit and talk he turned to face her,

"Would you be happy to live here love? It's not far out of Waterworth."

"Yes, I'm rapt in the character home, but I understand if we can't get it, we'll find something else." She nodded with a lump in her throat.

"Okay, I think it's good too, easy to maintain and perfect for the boat with easy access, so I'll get the agent." He nodded in agreement.

Sitting quietly in the car, the tension was extreme as he sent a text message to Penelope asking if she could come and see them in the car. A few minutes later she happily made her way over. Jonah got out of the car to meet her and explained that they were about to get married in February, so if they came to an agreement he would like a long settlement date if at all possible. Penelope said she didn't think that would be a problem as the vender was still looking for a home in a retirement village, there was often a waiting list to get into the best ones.

"So could we possibly get a settlement of 25th January?" he asked.

"I'll phone them." She moved out of hearing distance as Gemma waited with fingers crossed.

Jonah returned to the car again to sit with Gemma and update her that figures hadn't yet been discussed as he arranged a settlement date. He said it was a good bargaining tool instead of appearing too interested in the house.

Returning with a smile, Penelope was pleased to advise them, "They are happy to negotiate on the date and are actually relieved to have time to find somewhere."

"Oh that's great, I'm happy to pay the asking price of 1.8 million, I'll put down a 20% deposit so they know we're serious, with a settlement date close to our wedding date. I would like the home to be ready for my new wife to move into." Jonah negotiated.

Chapter 6

Penelope went inside away from listening distance to call the vendors, it was all agreed, they were pleased to accept the offer, she then returned to the car.

"The vendors are happy to stay a bit longer while they find a place, they will agree on the price and settlement date." Again reassuring him that she would have the paperwork signed later today.

"I'll get you to put my house and farm on the market in a few weeks' time, if it sells quickly then I'll have to move into one of my rentals until settlement date, but a buyer might be subject to selling his property first so let's get it all moving and signed up." Jonah said.

"If your place sells and the buyers want to move in, you can live with me at my cottage until this house is vacant." Gemma suggested if it would help to make the move easier.

The purchase offer agreement was filled in on top of the bonnet of the car, with an open space for settlement date being conditional on both vender and buyer agreement and she took the offer away to present to the vender.

"Can I come and see you at your home later tomorrow so I can do an appraisal on your farm?" asked Penelope.

"Yes, text me what time you're coming." Jonah nodded.

Gemma's stomach was full of butterflies as she sat quietly and watched it all unfold, this could be her new home, can it be true, is it possible and really happening.

"I need a drink now." She laughed nervously as Jonah returned to sit back in the driver's seat.

"It's good to do it straight away, this property is brilliant," he said. "I didn't want to miss out on it."

"So are you really going to sell the farm and your home?"

"Yes, I want to retire from working and just enjoy fishing and life with you."

"The good life eh?" smiling at him.

Penelope's text message broke the silence. The vender has already signed acceptance of the offer and terms. She arranged a time with Jonah to appraise his homestead tomorrow. On the drive home Gemma felt fatigued and full of nervous excitement and disbelief, it was all so surreal that today had actually happened and she was worn out. Jonah was surprisingly composed about leaving his home, he had found a boat ramp and a home to move forward with, and he was adamant about wanting to retire. Gemma also loves the new place and can't wait to live there. Although different, as it didn't have a beach for swimming, just tidal sea water coming and going up to the jetty, but the grounds and the big house were a dream come true.

The hydrangeas must look lovely when in full flower and how incredible lucky that the old couple had planted fruit trees when they built the house. Now they will have as much fruit as they need and won't miss Jonah's orchard, although they might want to plant some berry fruit. Gemma was very pleased with the decision to start anew.

The excitement was too much, an awesome day. Arriving at Jonah's he poured two glasses of bubbles for them to sit, relax and celebrate the finding of their new home, they were both ecstatically happy.

"Lucky we went to have a look today or we might have missed out on that lovely home. I suppose it's not everyone's cup of tea with a lot of lush lawn and trees to look after, but we can both do it together with a ride-on mower and we won't have anything else to do. Except you going fishing," Gemma laughed. "You can bring home the fish and I'll grow some potatoes for the chips." She joked cheerfully.

Sunday morning and Gemma's not in a hurry to go home, laying on his arm, waves of love and gratitude to know such a caring and generous man washed over her, and with subdued voices they whispered how lucky they were to have found each other.

Jonah touched her face with warm fingers and stroked her hair pondering over their discovery and dream for a future together. However, she knew that she needed to go home to come back down to earth.

She looked across the breakfast table at him, "I'll dust and vacuum through before I go, so it looks nice for the real-estate agent coming."

He stood up to remove the dishes, "You don't need to, just wipe the coffee table free of any dust if you want."

"I will do a quick clean. How are you feeling today, are you still happy to move?" Secretly hoping with fingers crossed he won't change his mind.

He appeared in front of her with a smile on his face looking like the cat that got the cream. "Yes, and this place will easily cover buying our home for us, then we can live a very good life and travel if you want!" He suggested.

Snuggling into his chest for a cuddle and smiling up at him, "I just want you to be happy, you deserve to retire, you have worked so hard to accumulate what you have."

"Having you in my arms forever will make me a very happy man." He says.

She pulled the vacuum cleaner out of the hallway cupboard, and after a quick flick around with the duster first, she then steps on the button to quickly hoover before putting it back into the cupboard.

"Well, I'm off home now darling, ring me tonight and tell me how you got on." She throw her bag into the car boot while Wilson waited to leap onto the back seat. Jonah reached into the car for a hug and a lingering kiss on her ready and waiting lips.

"I love you and I'm so glad we found a place that you will be happy to share with me," he whispered in her ear.

"I will love it there and I love you too, roll on wedding day so I don't have to go home. It'll be fine you'll see, oh and we'll need a fenced area for Wilson eh!"

"Well, that's a pleasant surprise to hear you say that!" and his lips again press gently on hers as he held her tightly, like he didn't want to ever let go. "It'll be easy to fence off the back yard for him, and of course there is plenty of room to run in the fruit trees. He'll be happy don't you worry love." Says Jonah.

"I'm over the moon with excitement and unable to worry. Bye for now." Jonah gently closed the car door.

The car roared into action, flying high on happiness this time she left without the compulsion to run away, as she had felt so often in the past.

Fifteen minutes later on arriving home she unpacked the car as usual, Wilson jumped down from the back seat only to sit staring at her, knowingly his brown eyes were pleading to take him for a walk to the beach.

"Okay, we can go for a walk, let me get your lead." He flew around in a circle while she slipped into a warm jacket, the weather was windy and she supposed it would be wild down at the beach.

They walked briskly, not only to keep warm but also because she didn't feel like a slow leisurely walk today, the only reason for going was to exercise Wilson. Arriving at the water's edge and looking out over the grey sea the horizon was blurred, an extraordinary sight of rough grey waves and the sky above the same blended grey, no rain just a very grey dismal day.

Gemma's inner world was not grey, something had changed from the desire for solitude that she once sort now completely absent, her thoughts were not on the wild waves as majestic as they were, the grey clouds dauntingly passing overhead didn't capture her attention either, as her heart and soul were monopolised with a longing to be with Jonah. She asked herself, what is this strange phenomenon, standing here in her favourite abandoned place, not feeling the peace, it was difficult to construe this detachment.

The crisp wind chilled her face fighting for recognition, Gemma was aware of some kind of disillusionment. Perhaps just tired, enthusiasm for the beach thwarted today. The bleak weather akin with her feelings as they walked quickly home, she had an urgency to phone him.

"Hi, it's just me." She wonders what to say.

"Hi, is everything okay?" came the concerned query.

"I'm missing you." She could hear a muffled giggle on the end of the line.

"How come? You only just left. He started to laugh.

Feeling embarrassed and a little silly she started to laugh as well.

"Well, I need to see you tomorrow, I don't know why, it could be I'm just too excited about everything that's happened. Finding a home together is pretty amazing and I'm unsettled. I need to be with you because everything is going to change for me again."

"Oh you're a funny one, of course you can come and stay anytime you want. I have farm work to do but there are always weeds to pull out in my garden if that makes you happy." He chuckled.

"I'll make a cup of tea and settle knowing that I'm seeing you in the morning. Bye darling."

"I love you, sleep tight and I'll see you tomorrow." A kind concern in his voice could be heard and it warmed her heart and lit up her world.

Gemma hung up and decided to cook an egg on toast for tea, which was all she could manage with her stomach all churned up. Oh, she remembers she has a book from the library to read. For some unknown reason her heart was beating faster, adrenaline charged.

"Dear Lord, please help me to calm down, I don't know what's wrong with me. Praise the lord for everything you are doing in my life."

Scooping Wilson's tinned dog food into his dish he scoffed it down and went off to bed quite happily after his brisk run. Gemma used the quiet time to enjoy wandering around her cottage garden as dusk settled in, finding it ecstatically pleasing and relaxing, followed by slumping in a comfy armchair to read the library book that had been waiting for a couple of days now, then she decided to have an early night.

The morning greeted her with cold and windy weather although she was grateful that it was not raining. Gemma was aware of an anxious sensation rushing through her entire body and a desperate need to see Jonah. She put it down to the upcoming big move from her home but she didn't delay, Wilson jumped into the car as soon as the door was opened for him and she throw in her gumboots, off they went. Rattle rattle sounded the tires as they crossed the cattle grid on arrival, she drove the car directly up to the front door, which was not open yet, that's unusual. Knocking on the door and waiting patiently for Jonah to respond she started to feel sick to her stomach. Intuition told her something was wrong, perhaps she was coming down with a bug or something.

No reply, she continued on around to the back door, only to find it was also closed and locked, now she was really feeling ill and needed to get into the house. Panic set in, while Wilson trailing on behind her finding the old wooden orchard gate open. So he ran ahead to play, Gemma had a quick look around through the gate, it was all cold, wet and miserable, Jonah nowhere to be seen. While Wilson was busy sniffing around it was a good chance for her to shut the gate and leave him safely in there until she felt better.

"Stay, good boy, I'll be back in a minute," she commanded assertively.

Gemma's energy levels swiftly roared into gear, every part of her was rushing as she went back to the car to fetch the gumboots she had left in the car boot. Leaving her shoes on the concrete drive she slid her feet into them and frantically proceeded down the race looking for Jonah. She wondered why the orchard gate was left open, and the house locked he must be outside somewhere. With her heart pounding and gut madly churning she knew something was not right. Rushing past a pile of fence battens lying on the ground Gemma thought to pick one up just in case of large roaming cattle.

Continuing on down the hill there was nothing out of the ordinary.

She frantically screamed out. "Jonah where are you!" even the cold air and wind felt airily quiet in hundreds of acres of paddocks.

On high alert Gemma's eyes combed what was up ahead of her, fear washing and dread crawling over her skin as she had a sense of readiness for roaming animals or whatever she may encounter. In the distance she can make out a paddock of about 30 cattle up ahead and she spots Jonah's bright yellow farm bike in the race. She was aware that she had to slow down, gumboots were not made for running and she was afraid of tripping up. Jonah needs her help she must not let him down and fortunately the race was dry, worn ground. Approaching the bike slowly, all the time keeping a look out for stampeding animals. Gemma's face flushed and panicked she noticed one gumboot clad foot sticking out from under long grass beside a broken fence. A group of cattle were standing beside the long grass under which he lay. What can she do?

Taking time to quickly look around, trying not to startle the animals she observed a gate down the far end of the paddock, leading into the race, with an empty paddock opposite it, which also had a gate into the race.

Tightly gripping the batten Gemma ran up to the gate, with her heart pounding gradually opened the spare paddock, which was adjacent to Jonah's, she was frantic to get to him and prayed that he was alive. Cautiously she opened the paddock where the cattle stood menacingly watching her, working steadily she had to do this.

Always being careful to stay behind one gate, she then joined the two paddocks together. Another quick prayer, that the cattle would be tempted to eat fresh grass in a new paddock, *please oh please let it work.*

"Oh Lord, I have to get to Jonah," she whispered quietly under her breath.

"Come on, come on." Gemma called out as loudly as she could trying to remain calm and assertive to the animals. They turn to face her, with one starting to move forward towards her, slowly hesitantly the others followed, arriving at the gate their huge dark eyes weighting her up. Her hands were dripping wet with nervous tension, this was so new and dangerous for her to be attempting, but she had no choice. The cattle appeared unsure whether to leave the old paddock, suddenly she remembers the fence paling still gripped firmly in her hand and walking back keeping within the safety of the race, to what could be seen of Jonah, still no movement.

Gemma lifted the batten waving, and started yelling, "Whoa, whoa go on get out of here." She was almost screaming at them.
With all the hollering and aggressive movement of the batten, she hoped they would be wary and not what to grapple with her.

The first 500kg animal left the paddock and ran across into fresh pasture, slowly they all started to find the courage to run in as they follow each other. Her heartbeat was pounding in her throat, her stress levels were high, with beads of perspiration appearing on her skin after confronting the massive animals, and all the time frantic to get Jonah to safety. She was impatient to see if he was breathing. After the last beast was out of his paddock and they had moved off away from the connected gates, she quietly, cautiously walked up and locked them in the new pasture. Thank goodness, breathing a sigh of relief now she can help her love, her fearful heart hadn't stopped pounding but the nausea was completely gone. No time for that as she ran over to Jonah.

"Jonah," she yelled and tapped on his shoulder, he appeared unharmed, then she saw it. As she pulled the grass away from his head, a red puddle on the ground and blood still dripping into it, where from? Suddenly realizing, she didn't have her cell phone with her.

"Jonah, can you move?" she yelled at him in panic, he stirred and groaned as she shakes his shoulder harder out of fear.

"Oh, my head hurts." He stirred, as he opened his eyes.

"Can we get you onto the bike?" Gemma asked, all the time confident that he could, he had to as the farm bike was the quickest way forward.

"Yeah I think so, I'm a bit dizzy," he managed to pull himself into a sitting position, both of them being careful not to touch any wires that may still be live from the electric fence.

"I'll squish in next to you and steer, we'll go slowly back to the house." Reaching for her clean folded handkerchief, glad that she always kept one in her pocket. Gemma pressed it to the cut now very obvious on his head with blood still trickling down the side of his face.

"Keep pushing on that," she instructed him while putting his hand onto the cloth. Somehow he sat side saddle across the centre raised area of the bike and she got on the other side; thank goodness it started first time. She had never driven a farm bike before, and it was scary and difficult to drive while running on adrenalin.

"Hold on to the back rail with your other hand, here we go," she cried out. "Let's get you home."

Slowly they began to move off, with Gemma silently praying that Jonah wouldn't faint or fall off. She reluctantly kept her speed down, although under pressure to get Jonah there safely and as quickly as possible. Incredibly, they made it to the back door of his house, and she fumbled around in his trouser pocket to find the house key to get inside. She helped him off the bike, with her arm linked under his he wasn't heavy as he was still able to stand. Half falling and half climbing off, he moved to the lounge and thankfully collapsed into an armchair, still holding the blood soaked handkerchief to his head, with blood now oozing through between his fingers.

"You're okay, just relax I'll grab the phone," she ordered him.

Running to the phone and dialling 111, "Ambulance please."

Chapter 7

Gemma was feeling a bit out of breath and realized that in the panic she had been holding her breath and was now also quite dizzy, she gulped in a big breathe of air and sighed before she fell down. It had been very stressful, and she carefully gave the official on the other end of the phone a calm explanation of the address before going back to Jonah.

"It's on the way, are you okay?" she asked him.

"The animals will be loose," he said anxiously. "And the fence is down."

Sitting beside him, she patted his thigh while explaining, "No don't worry, I've put them into another paddock, they have plenty of fresh food in there as well as being secure. It's all okay. Do you remember what happened?" she asked.

"I can't remember, just that I saw the fence post leaning on an angle so I think I was trying to straighten it. Then a No.8 wire broke and flew up at me, I must have fallen in the trench and hit my head on the post, perhaps I got an electric shock? I don't remember much, until I heard you yelling, and saw all the cattle standing around and looking down at me."

The siren sounding in the driveway contributed to an alarming urgency, "The ambulance is here." Gemma exclaimed looking up.
She rushed over to open the front door and let the paramedic in, pointing to where Jonah was seated.

"He's over there, I found him in the paddock with a cut on his head, a bit confused and was unconscious when I found him," she blurted out the explanation.

Carrying a bag, the paramedic walked over to assess Jonah, "Okay, well I'll dress that wound until we get you to hospital, then you'll probably need a stitch in it, anything else hurt?" he questioned Jonah.

"No, I don't think so, I'm a bit dizzy though," Jonah says as he is guided towards the ambulance, once settled they quickly headed off and she locked the house before following on in her car.

Time inched along invisibly as the hands on the clock never seemed to move at all, they wait in emergency to see a doctor. Gemma thought about Wilson, he would be wondering where she was. They sat holding hands and didn't talk much, the stark white walls contrasted by many colourful plastic chairs, it was an uncomfortable silence as people sat around the room tolerating pain. Accidents are a sobering occurrence before this sequence of events ever unfolds. No one plans for an accident and the lack of sound in the room was profound, while everyone pondered over how their circumstances would change. Gemma's heart rate had normalized and Jonah seemed okay, except for the cut to his head. She was aware of the antiseptic smells burning her nose.

"I hope you can go home tonight," she whispered, (it seemed inappropriate to speak loudly in the hospital surroundings.)

"Should be able to," he squeezed her hand. "Lucky you came and found me." His voice sounding a mix of emotions touched Gemma's heart.

"You'll be okay, everything's good."

The nurse calls out "Jonah Frederick."

They both stand to follow her quietly into the doctor's office. Jonah was asked about what happened, and the nurse entered with a bowl of intravenous injections, cotton wool swabs and antiseptic.

"Will you need a tetanus shot," she asked as she started to tidy up the cut on his head.

"That's up to date, because I have a farm," he replied.

"Right, well it looks like you were knocked out and have a concussion, so we want to keep you here tonight to keep an eye on you," interjects the doctor from his desk. "It should be okay to go home tomorrow, you'll be contacted about a follow up visit and it will be explained about any help you might need at home," he said while making notes on the file.

Jonah flinched as the cut was stitched, the reality of his situation appearing to be just hitting home as he seemed to wither before her eyes, like a flower on a scorching hot day. All she wanted to do was take him home and care for him but he needed to rest, so silently she made the decision to only stay with him until after having had a comforting cup of tea together, then she excused herself explaining that she would be back in the morning.

"I've left my phone number as your contact person so they can ring me if need be, will you be okay? You look really tired!" smiling across the bed at him sitting up in his funny old-man hospital pyjamas.

"Yeah, I wish I could go home with you, I'm okay."

"Everyone wants to go home from hospital but it's only for one night. I'll pick up some clean clothes for you before I go home tonight. Wilson is still running around in your orchard wondering what's happened to us. I'll feed your cat tonight before going home."

"Thanks love." He reached out his hand toward her, his arms outstretched with antiseptic smells even worse on the ward. Looking up at her, so helpless and loveable.

While kissing, he held on unnecessarily tightly, evidence of his sullen state of vulnerability. Gemma reluctantly pulled away, proceeding back to the comfort of her little white Honda, with shaking hands she fumbled in her old handbag for the car keys. She slumped down into the car seat, pressed the lock on the drivers door in need of security and rest, she was suddenly overwhelmed by the events of the day.

A flood of cold tears ran unrestrained down her frozen face, her nose was wet, and as she accepted this moment as the conclusion to a very stressful day she let it wash over her. Courage gave way to tears.

Gemma began to pray, giving thanks for sending her to help Jonah, thanks for assisting her to move the cattle away and praise for preventing Jonah from being trampled. What might have happened was not worth thinking about. She gave thanks for the urgency and courage she had to find him, and most of all she praised the Lord that Jonah was alive.

Gemma was unaware of how long she sat recalling the past, remembering when her first husband sustained a serious head injury, she felt the horror of it ever happening again. Jonah has hit his head but they said it was just a cut and that he had concussion. Struggling to be sensible, the tenson was mounting, she knew that a lot of people who have had concussion, it didn't always lead to dementia.

"Please Lord don't let my past repeat itself, let Jonah be okey." Gemma wiped away the tears and started the car, she needed a cuddle with her dog, and a good night's sleep was required so they could put today behind them. Everything would be alright tomorrow when she returned to take her man home.

"Here I am Wilson," she called out, opening the orchard gate.

He came bounding over happy to greet her with full body wagging and jumping all over her with dirty feet, but she didn't care.

He's well! allowing him to jump into the familiar back seat of the only car he has ever known, closing the car door with her companion her stomach settled. She was thankful that he was such a good dog quietly waiting patiently for someone to return to fetch him. Running back inside the house Gemma anxiously filled Jonah's backpack with clean underwear, jeans and shirt and remembering the most important thing before going home, to leave a dish of cat food out in the barn. Emotionally exhausted, she longed to be home and she drove as the effect of fatigue started to take over, reinforcing her desire to just have a quick microwaved tea and off to bed early, what a day.

As soon as light filtered through into the bedroom she leapt out of bed powerless to wait, even though the doctor would not do his discharge rounds until about 10am. She couldn't wait to get to the hospital to see how Jonah was, the separation was unbearable.

"Let's go around the park early today Wilson, to fill in a bit of time for me eh?"

The mere mention of the park and he ran off to the garage to get his lead, all is right with his world. It is a cold July morning and she is grateful the weather is fine, although the days are noticeably shorter now, the hours of light fewer. As the two of them stroll down the snaking footpath towards the sea, they walked past houses with the drapes still closed, the smell of last night's chimney smoke was a comforting retrospection of warmth as the woodsy smell lingered heavily under slow moving dark clouds, a promise of imminent rain. Some rain is needed to fill everyone's water tanks, but hopefully not while Wilson and her are out walking.

The magic of this place, and even the smell of the stinky seaweed on the white sand churned up in last night's stormy seas, provided her and Wilson with a hushed peace and tranquillity once more. The moment she moved here she was aware of the spiritual sanctuary it afforded her and she didn't think she would ever completely give it up. It has been a place of healing and of bringing her closer to the universe, she began to appreciate that people need people and she no longer wanted to be a recluse anymore. Although wanting to live with Jonah, she's passionate about Latent Beach and will always keep this place in her heart to return to, from time to time.

Blinking quickly to clear the tears from her eyes, she psychologically blamed it on the crisp sea air, blurring her sight as she admired how much Wilson had grown and had become a wonderful little friend and companion. The two of them enjoyed the open air and the sound of Tui twittering in the treetops, Fantails swoop down fearlessly close to her as they soar around looking for any little bit of sun's rays to warm themselves. Wilson's speed accelerated, feeling liberated without his lead on, lengthy, strong legs barely touching the ground he glided effortlessly, watching him a smile spread across Gemma's face. Pleased that she could provide him with such freedom.

"Come Wilson," she called. He appeared at her feet in lightening time. "What a good dog," she says to him as the warmth of love encompassed her entire body.

Leaving him at home settled with his bone he was content to rest after his exercise, she set off to the hospital wondering what she would be confronted with. Rushing through what seemed like never ending hospital corridors until she arrived at Ward 5. Looking along the corridor to find Jonah's name printed, one of four tiny names slotted into place on the wall right beside double smoke stop doors.

A hint of fear filling her as she hoped he was allowed to go home. Gemma found him sitting up reading and waiting in those funny pyjamas.

"Morning darling how are you?" she called out cheerfully.

"I have a headache but apart from that I'm okay, the doc said I can go home and see my own doctor next week." He spoke a little slower than need be.

Relieved, she had trouble restraining the compulsion to fling her arms around him but opted for a reserved kiss on his mouth instead, aware of others in the ward looking on.

"I'll go and check with the office; here are your clothes to put on." Placing the backpack on the bedside chair. "I put your socks and shoes in the other side of the bag for you." She smiled into his eyes while zapping the drape around the track, creating a disturbance in a hushed place where everyone spoke quietly, she eagerly headed for the office.

Approaching the reception desk, "Can I take Jonah Frederick in Ward 5 home this morning?" she asked.

The nurse didn't look up from the computer, nodded and informed her doctor has signed the discharge forms, he's ready to go.

Rushing back to the ward she found Jonah dressed and sitting in the chair, pulling shoes on and joking with the others about escaping.

"That was quick, don't rush with a headache, take it easy and I'll carry the bag with your washing in it." Putting her hand on his back guiding him to stand up, she was relieved that he appeared fine.

The drive to the farm was quiet as he seemed tired, and dozed off, rattle rattle and he woke up to the familiar sound and vibrating shudder of the cattle grid.

"You sit down and I'll make a nice cup of tea; I've brought lemon tarts from home."

"That sounds good love," he smiled. "I'm feeling better after having some painkillers with breakfast, they've kicked in now."

Sitting inside Jonah was able to relax in his soft padded recliner chair, and after a cuppa together she began to insist that he was not to go outside. Gemma reassured him that she would feed the cat again and the deer and cattle have plenty of grass, there's no need for him to venture down to the paddocks today.

"I'll have to see what's happened to the fence!" he pleaded.

"Not now you don't, it can wait until tomorrow. There are no animals lose anywhere so just have one day to rest and get better." Trying to impress on him the importance of what had happened.

"Well, you're putting your foot down bossy!" he said with a smile.

"Yes well, you were very lucky, it could have been far worse and you have a concussion to get over so be sensible." Again strongly insisting.

"I just want to sit here and watch some sport on television." He smiled aware of his sore head.

"Good idea, I've left some sandwiches ready beside your chair and I'll take out a frozen pie for the microwave for tea. I'm going home after I feed the cat so you can rest, that's the best thing for you. See you tomorrow okay." She crossed the room to give him a kiss.

"Sounds good because I am tired and actually don't feel much like company."

"I know, that's okay you look completely shattered, promise you won't go outside eh!"

"No. I'll be good, see you tomorrow love." He planted a respectable kiss on her lips before saying goodbye once more. Letting herself out, locking the front door as she went to feed the cat.

She drove through the cold torrential rain that had been threatening to arrive all morning, Gemma turned on the car heater, the downpour hit with a passion, turbulent and thunderous flashes of lightening shot like bullets overhead and reluctantly she slowed down. Frantic, all she wanted was to get home as quickly as possible out of the lightening. However, the turmoil of bits of tree branches and leaves flying around instilled fear, it was scary so she tried to focus on just getting home in one piece, no matter how long it took. Wilson needed her and she hoped he was not afraid of the thunder. At least she had the reassurance that there was no way Jonah would be tempted to check on his animals in the storm. Arriving home safely Wilson greeted her with a grand slurpy welcome and they settled in for an afternoon of listening to music and reading a book.

The days turned into a month and Jonah seemed to be back to his normal self, and keen to head back into dancing. They both agreed to go and only have one slow Rock n roll together just so they could socialize. When they arrived at the massive glass doors there was a red head woman hovering around the doorway, Gemma gave Jonah a questioning look and he shook his head, he didn't know her but she followed them to the table they sat at and introduced herself as Jane. Sitting down opposite, she deliberately leaned over all the time to flirt with Jonah, laughing and showing her cleavage she leaned in to talk, flaunting her obviously fake eyelashes and sticking out her oversized top-heavy breasts. She harassed them with many questions about what he did for a living, and then of course all about the farm and how much land he had. Batting her lashes as she starred into his eyes and speaking every word drawn out with her Botox lope-sided lips. They both acted politely towards her thinking perhaps she had been drinking.

Jonah prompted. "Let's dance darling." Rising from his seat at the same time as speaking, he asked without waiting for a reply. Gemma gladly nodded and followed him.

"Thank goodness you asked me to dance I'm so bored with that fake woman drawling all over you." Gemma complained.

Laughing he agreed and explained that he often came upon women that were only after someone with money, he was used to it and found it sickening. Explaining how one actually told him once that she wanted to find a man with money, because she didn't want to work anymore.

"Oh my goodness," shocked, Gemma exclaimed, "I couldn't marry for money or burden myself with someone I didn't love. Life can be horrible even with money."

"Gold diggers don't have the brains to think of what the outcome might be, they only dream about all the stuff they want to buy, believing that will make them happy. It doesn't. You can still be very lonely and miserable if you're with the wrong person," he says gently looking down at her held tightly in his arms.

The music started, then she noticed he was doing too many repetitions of the same dance moves over and over, which was out of character for him. When she queried him, he explained he couldn't remember anymore moves, she gently guided him off the dance floor to stand at a round table with bar stools.

Jonah went to get two iced pineapple juices for them both, only to stand around avoiding Jane until she left to dance with someone. They were then able to return to their table with Gemma's coat hanging over the back of her chair. Settled, they began to socialize and have a nice time catching up with Jack and Pauline, a couple who they have seen many times in the past. In due course deciding to leave early. Backing out of the carpark she turned to watch through the cars back window, concerned that perhaps not everything was back to normal after all!

"Stop!" yelled Gemma as he sped out and was about to run into a parked car behind him. He stopped thank goodness and looked over at her bewildered.

"There's a car behind you; you nearly hit it," she exclaimed.

"I didn't see it there; lucky you stopped me!" he said.
Starting to accelerate again they continued on their way enjoying the drive on a beautiful fine evening. He continued straight through a red light, a loud horn blast startled Gemma.

"What's he going on about?" Jonah said indignantly.

"You went through a red light," she explained, shaken.

"Did I? I didn't see it." He gasped in panic.

Gemma sat nervously observing him all the way home to arrive at their destination safely, and when Sunday morning Jonah woke up complaining that he felt a bit dizzy; That was when they looked at each other and knew that something was wrong.

"I'll make an appointment to see the doctor next week." he promised.

"You're still a bit tired and dizzy. I'm a bit worried about you."

"Yeah," nodding his head in agreement. "I'll get a check-up and find out about the headaches as well."

"Thanks darling." She kissed and hugged him; he was obviously not well. Gemma decided she should go home and let him rest.

Chapter 8

Life continued on and Gemma was back enjoying the beauty of the sea again, it was her place of peace and seclusion for her to think. Gemma anxiously awaited Jonah's results from the doctor, (he's been referred to the hospital). While waiting for that appointment other things became apparent, the niggling headaches that should have improved by now were being masked by the number of painkillers he was taking, and his vision was weird as he missed things, his aim was off. Jonah insisted on going to the hospital appointment alone so she waited anxiously for the evening phone call.

Seven o'clock arrived and the phone rang. "Hello, how did you get on at the hospital today?" was her first comment, an anxious response.

"Well, I'll explain it all to you tomorrow, can you come around?" he requested.

"Of course, is something wrong?"
Oh no, her body fills with trepidation, blood rushed to make her heartbeat loudly, why won't he talk over the phone.

"Yes, and they found a slow recognition with my eyesight so that's why I didn't see the red light when I was driving it was because of a delay."

"Oh, can they fix it?" she asked with bated breath.

"Well, that's what I want to talk with you about tomorrow, not now on the phone, but there is a procedure."

"I've been waiting all day to hear from you so Wilson and I walked to the beach, the park and then spent time in my garden this afternoon, it was cold but the spring bulbs are coming up now." She tried to chat light heartedly like nothing was wrong while her eyes filled with tears.

"That's good, well it was a bit traumatic at the hospital today so I won't talk much tonight." He said quietly.

"Okay darling everything will be okay," she tried to reassure him without knowing what the problem was. They said goodbye and she hung up the phone, before going to make a cup of tea, concluding that bang on the head must have been more serious than they first realized.

Driving along the winding road her mind was crammed with alarm bells ringing and the burning acid felt deep in her gut was horrid. Whatever is looming they will face it together. Arriving at his house the front door is ajar, which was a welcome relief, unlike the last time. Gemma had left Wilson at home today as she wouldn't stay long.

"Hi, just me," she called out.

"I'm in the kitchen love, putting on the jug." Came the reply as he walked around the corner where she could see him. "You might need a coffee because I have something to discuss with you," he said as he wrapped his arms around Gemma.

"What's wrong? I'm really getting concerned now." She kissed him, holding on like she never wanted to let him go. This can't be happening.

"Let's take these out in the garden to talk." Gemma followed along, sitting beside the beautiful ferns growing in the sheltered area, he looked into her eyes and began to explain.

"After I complained about the headaches, dizziness and impaired vision they did an MRI scan at the hospital and found I have Hydrocephalus, which is water on the brain. It's most common in children and those over 60 years old. The usual way to correct it is to put a shunt into my body to draw the extra fluid away, meaning a 2-4 day hospital stay. But because I've only had a problem since the head injury the doctor has suggested rather than go through a permanent shunt, I should try removal of cerebrospinal fluid with a lumber puncture to be done first to see if symptoms are relieved." Jonah slumped in his chair, like a bouncy castle that someone had just let all the air out of. "Hopefully then I will return to normal."

They both had a sip of coffee and considered this before Jonah continued. "There's only a small chance it might fix it; what do you think I should do? I wanted us to discuss it together as you are my life and my future wife, any procedure needs to be considered together."

"I hear that lumber punctures are painful but surely its worth trying, even with only a small chance of success. Hopefully withdrawing fluid it may not return too much as your head heals," she considered that was what she would do if it were her.

"How successful is a shunt?" Gemma cautiously asked.

"If a shunt is inserted into a ventricle to drain fluid away and the surgery is successfully I'll have a normal life span. If we don't release the fluid from my brain it is fatal, something must be done." He spoke very matter of fact but with an causal tone of nervous upset.

"I'd opt for not panicking, try the lumber puncture to remove fluid and pressure, wait and pray you'll return to how you were before the accident," Gemma suggested as they sat facing each other, with eyes full of dread.

"I'm glad you said that, because I needed a second opinion, being in this serious position I'm afraid I might not behave rationally or perhaps rush into it, before I have any loss of co-ordination or get cognitive difficulties." he exhaled with a huge sigh of relief that now she knew the situation.

"We'll watch it and if withdrawing fluid doesn't help your headache go away then you have to rethink the situation." She smiled and tried to reassure him.

"Thanks love for being here with me I'm sorry this has happened." His chin scrunched up as he made a *what next* face.

"It can't be helped, and whichever way we will get you right again. Christmas is just around the corner eh!" she attempted to sound positive and lighten the severity of his health issue.

"I love you," he declares looking on with blurry eyes.

"I love you too, it's just a hic cup along the way, and that's why we have each other. You won't go through anything on your own I'll be at the hospital with you. Well now that's sorted, lets go for a lie down together," she gave a cheeky giggle.

"Don't forget I have a headache."

"It is the woman that always says that, not the man," she retorted.

They were both relieved, a decision had been made and the tension eased, as they walked towards the bedroom the heavy weight of worry had been shared.

Lying on the bed together, immersed in the closeness of a loving relationship having each other, it completed and warmed Gemma's inside, Jonah was so affectionate and patient. She stretched out on top of the bed not wanting to be demanding, just happy to be there for him. His arm reaching across Gemma's body as he kissed her, and the need for restraint was strong, desire although awareness of his health uppermost in their minds. Lying beside each other filled her heart and soul and she was mindful of this special loving moment, his finger gently ran down her cheek and followed the outline of her lips, sending pleasant quivers down her body.

Looking beyond his eyes delving deeper than the obvious, his softness as a person, a gentle soul who had become her best friend. His hand glided and explored as breathing quickened, what a wonderous thing that one small word, **love!** an emotion felt from a connection with someone, when just that look, a depth of passion and caring combine in a world without time or space, a superior consciousness of a miraculous phenomenon not everyone encounters in their lives.

Two people understanding without words and connecting in mind, it was the ultimate zenith. Holding her close to him Jonah lay still in each other arms, breathing slowly they both dozed off. Rousing a short while later Gemma didn't want to leave and he didn't want her too either, but realistically he needed rest and to her that superseded everything for now. Pulling herself out of the dozy relaxed wonderland she resolved to get off the bed.

"I'll have a look in your cupboard and see what you have for lunch."

He rouses and smiles. "Sorry I fell asleep, I'm relaxed with you here and it relieves my headache."

"Do you know what you feel like for lunch?" she smiled kindly with her hand resting on his muscular arm.

"There should be some crackers, cheese, tomatoes and pickled onions there," Jonah replied.

"Great I'll get a platter made up and we can have a picnic on top of the bed together."

"That'll be nice." Smiling he gripped her hand giving it a little squeeze.

Laying several slices of tasty cheese and slices of juicy tomatoes in rows on a long white serving platter she heaped crispy round crackers with some sliced pickles beside them on the other half of the plate. It doesn't take long before heading back to the bedroom to prop a pillow behind Jonah's head, encouraging him to stay in bed.

The delicious looking platter of finger food was easy to eat nestled between them as Gemma pulled over the ecru coloured bedroom chair and sat facing him. They helped themselves, topping the crackers and laying them on two small plates she had brought in.

Gemma's heart warmed to watch him smile, it was a pleasure to look after Jonah. Telling herself not to worry, everything would work out this time.

"I'm going to phone the doctor this afternoon and tell him I'm going ahead with the lumber puncture," he said. "It only takes an hour, and apparently I have to stay lying down for a bit to stabilize the pressure. When they take the fluid out they'll check to see if there's any blood in it, fingers crossed there's not!"

"There won't be, you seem to be quite well except for the hydrocephalus. Do you need me to do anything before I go home?" she asked.

"No, I've been out and fed the shed cat this morning and I feel better after our talk. I wish you could stay." He had livened up now.

"Me too, but you need to rest. I'm a phone call away, it will all come right. I'm sure the knock caused the fluid on the brain and if they remove some, once everything has healed fingers crossed you won't need any invasive surgery." She tried to instil some positivity as there was no point thinking the worst.

"I've made some head way with subdivision up north on my holding and the fencing is being started next week," he says as he changed the subject.

Sitting down on the bed for a few minutes, she let him talk about the process of selling and the protective covenant on the land, before reaching down to join moist lips for a long, sensuous kiss.

"Ring me tonight darling if you feel up to it and tell me how you get on with the doctor," whispering into his ear before standing to leave. "Bye, talk to you later."

Wandering to the kitchen she washed and dried the platter and put it away before gathering her car keys.

"Okay I will. Bye love," he called from the bedroom as her car keys rattled on the way to the solid wooden front door.

Arriving home drained of energy as though the plug had been pulled out. After greeting Wilson she left him in the backyard to play by himself for a little longer, she needed some restorative time on her own. Slipping her arms into her warm beach jacket she lifted from the hook in the laundry she wanted to let her mind and body meander while she walked along the seaside, longing to breath in the coolness of fresh air.

Deep in thought she convinced herself that she wasn't worried, although anything to do with the brain conjured up memories of her past life when her husband had an aneurism and brain surgery. Their lives changed forever as he became a different person, she had a fear of history repeating itself. Turning the corner the magnificent sight of white sand beneath mirror-still cool blue sea, and the greenness of paddocks as a backdrop on the other side of the water captivated her. Gemma knew that there can be no substitute for the ocean, sometimes wild and other times calm, like a living thing with a mind of its own, it continued on unrestrained.

Striding along the water's edge in her well-worn beach shoes oblivious to the salt laden cold, soaking through her socks and freezing her toes, she wanted to feel, something. Engaging in the freedom and pausing to admire this oasis of peace and tranquillity Gemma trusted that she was not alone, everything would be okay this time. Squelching all the way home, Wilson was pleased to see her and instantly dropped a ball at her feet, his huge brown eyes enquiringly inspecting her.

"Okay fella I'll just get dry feet and then we'll play."

Looking up at the clock on the wall, it was nearing seven o'clock, will he phone or was he too sick?" A shrill sounds from her mobile.

Gemma hurried to answer it, with a rush of blood through her body she was pleased to hear from him.

"Hi, are you feeling better?" she cried out, anxious to hear his gruff voice.

"Pretty much the same, but my doctor got me an appointment for next Wednesday to have the lumber puncture procedure."

"That's great news, I'll take you." Faking a cheerfulness for his benefit.

"Thanks love, it won't take long."

Tuesday came along quite quickly, and tomorrow it would happen. Gemma contemplated how challenging it had been leaving Jonah to manage the cattle on his own, not wanting to interfere simply unable to stop herself. She continually stressed to him he could leave them in a fresh paddock for a bit longer and not move them as often, and he was definitely not allowed to fix any fences until he was well.

Waking to a gorgeous spring day with a very high tide, as Wilson and Gemma decide on a walk, they stand on the pier and watch two boat trailers backing down to the water's edge, one expensive looking boat was carefully manoeuvring around the other much loved boat that had a humble unpainted plywood roof. Dad was treading water as two little girls stood on shore watching, once he had the boat in the water he called them over. The eldest with her masses of blonde curls bouncing off her shoulders happily ran into the water and dad heaved her up and onto the boat. The younger of the two appearing to be around three years old seemingly reluctant to get her gumboots wet, shuffling her feet and waiting with arms outstretched.

Good old dad to the rescue swishes over in his tall gumboots to fetch her, hoisting her onto one hip and plopping her into the boat with her sister, two little floral sunhats and a boat full of smiles all round. The three looked so happy with dad disconnecting the trailer winch before he drove the truck up to park in the carpark. He looked to be a week-end dad spending time with his girls.

People eagerly watching, the early sunrise warmth could now be felt heated on her face, the clear sea was peaceful, with no waves or wind to ruffle it, while sparkles of light flickered and bounce off the top of the water and she anticipated that they would have a wonderful carefree day.

Continuing on her way through scattered Puhutakawa trees, reaching the old park bench where she sat snatching time to contemplate her concern over the hospital visit and remembering the haunting vision of Jonah perplexed about his headaches, and of his look of relief when she didn't freak out, offering to be with him while the doctor drew out some fluid. His face had searched for reassurance, her mind replaying that lost look over and over. Gemma felt sure that the procedure would level out the pressure and he would go back to normal without any further intervention. She lowered her head to pray that would be the case.

Her mobile rang and she was quick to answer it. "Hi darling are you taking things quietly?" she inquires.

"Oh yes, actually I can't wait for tomorrow to see if it sorts me out, I'm wanting to get it over with." He says.

"I'll pick you up at 8am to give us plenty of time because you know how unpredictable the traffic can be," Gemma suggested.

"Sounds good, I'll be ready."

Gemma could feel the tense pause; he did not have any more to say. Jonah was keen for their plans for the future to proceed, the tension ran down the line like a pulse spurting blood through a vein and there was nothing more that could be said. They both waited with crossed fingers and hopeful hearts for their future plans.

"See you in the morning." Gemma said with as much cheer as possible.

"Yep, bye love." He called back before setting the receiver into its cradle.

A shudder and resulting goose bumps ran down her arms as she put another log on the fire, the days had been beautiful, but the nights were still cool, with the added airy darkness of possible outcomes tomorrow pressing heavily on her mind.

The traffic flowed quickly and finding the day surgery building was easy, she focused on driving and Jonah pointed out a parking space. Slowly gliding into park, they got out of the car and Gemma pulled the backpack out of the car boot. The nurse had instructed Jonah to bring it, saying it was just in case of a delay and he needed an unwanted overnight stay, hopefully not, as they have an early appointment leaving plenty of daytime for his recovery.

"Jonah Frederick, follow me please," came the call from a white clad nurse.

"See you later darling," she kissed him on the cheek in the waiting room. "I'll go and enjoy a hot chocolate while you have fun, and I'll see you later," she joked with a nervous smile.

"Yeah right, see you later." He gave Gemma a tight hug, picking up his backpack.

The hospital café was too clinical, even the pleasant aromatic smell of coffee could not mask the antiseptic environment. Gemma ordered a takeaway hot chocolate and decided on a walk to the local park to wait alone, gloomily watching the ducks. Little bundles of sleek glossy feathers floated on the surface of the lily pond, grossly overfed by visitors the ducks sat motionless, encircled by a musty odour of ageing bread. Feeling anxious, her cold hands wrapped around the paper cup seeking a little warmth, it was comforting and drew her attention away from thoughts of what's happening back at the hospital. Tugging the plastic lid off the cup, a comforting chocolaty aroma filled her nostrils and she slurped off the luscious frothy top to get to the smoothness of the rich chocolate liquid beneath. The sweet warmth was mildly comforting as while trying not to worry, she whispered her prayer. *'Dear Lord, please let withdrawing cerebral fluid fix Jonah.'*

Eventually strolling back to the hospital and finding the waiting room the nurse came up to her.

"Jonah is resting and it went well. The doctor said to tell you that there was no blood in the fluid. He's very happy and we just have to wait and see if the hydrocephalus levels will normalize now that some fluid has been removed."

Chapter 9

The good news extinguished her burning nervous stomach as she exhaled, like a breath of wind blowing out a candle.

"Thank you, can I see him?" Gemma asked.

"Yes you can, but he has to remain lying flat for a bit longer before going home." The nurse warned.

"Okay, thank you." The nurse lead her through a couple of doors to find Jonah lying down. He looked very handsome, like a movie star his face freshly shaven this morning and with short, styled hair, the classy farmer. Gemma was satisfied with the outcome so far and was so happy to see Jonah.

Once allowed to leave the hospital they headed straight home, and Jonah straight away headed down the hallway towards the bedroom, he needed to lie down.

She called out to him. "Do you feel like eating anything?"

"Just a cuppa and some of your homemade chocolate biscuits you brought with you." He smiled, after seeing them in the car.

"I'll bring a small plate full and a bowl of mandarins to have next to the bed, the more you lie down the better for everything to settle at the moment," she called back to him.

Flopping down onto the side of his bed, she flung her arms around his neck, and the tears of relief started to slide from under closed eye lids, they ran down her face and she felt silly.

"Hey, it's alright, I'm okay," he uttered with affection, his hand rubbing her back.

With emotions running high and not really sure why she got upset, Gemma was just glad that that was over.

While minutes pass in a heart-warming embrace with neither of them speaking they sat, and after a wee while, they started to share feelings to each other, hugging and expressing how they both want to move on quickly with their life together. Deciding to put Jonah's house and farm on the market straight away, and if it sells before getting into their new home in February, then he will move into her spare room until after the wedding. Not wanting to waste any more time apart. Life really was too short and every year seemed to disappear faster than the last one.

"You sleep and I'll be back this afternoon to get tea and stay the night." Gemma smiled.

Not waiting for a reply as she walked towards the door and drove home to the beach. Entering her cottage by the sea she was overwhelmed with gratitude; she loved this haven. This home had afforded her peace, healing and security over the years, walking through to her new kitchen built to her design she loved so much, she was surprised at how it suddenly felt very hollow, the solitude she once craved now rendering an emptiness. Gemma was jostled out of her thoughts as she became aware of the warm hairy body rubbing up against her bare legs. She wasn't alone as she bent to wrap her arms around her faithful friend, relinquishing the making of a hot drink, now replaced by a desire for a walk to the beach, their beach.

A thundering tide with crashing waves leaping up the sea wall, Gemma had seen taller waves, but these were low and more forceful with creamy foam being stirred up, adhering to the tops of the wall like the hot frothy milk sticking around the edge of a coffee cup. Clear crisp sea air filled her lungs and blew away any anxiety left from the hospital trip. The return to hospital corridors with their distinctive smells and sounds of clatter had been more stressful than she had realized. Although her emotional wounds from her past had healed, she was left with scars, the memory of her deceased husband going through brain surgery, distressing moments still surfaced occasionally.

The sky's angry grey clouds with shades of pink pushing through any gap was bizarre, the environment at Latent Beach never ceased to amaze, with its untamed beauty.

Gemma and Wilson took time to wander around the garden before heading back to the farm. On the drive, deciding to stop at the butchers on the way to get a couple of nice pork chops as a treat for Jonah tonight, cooking a lovely dinner for the two of them was now her plan.

"Hi, it's just us," she called out while turning the unlocked door handle. Jonah came striding towards her with a huge smile, a smile that suggested he felt better.

"My headaches gone!" he grinned.

Elated, with moist eyes. "Oh that's great news, let's hope it stays away eh." After speaking, Gemma wished she hadn't said her thoughts out loud.

"Do you have time to relax in the spa for a while before putting on the tea?" he asked with his arms firmly wrapped around her and pleading grey eyes gazing down.

"Yes I think that would be okay, but no alcohol until you get out of the water, just in case you faint or something." She mused.

He laughed, enjoying the fact that someone cared, slipping his arms around Gemma's slim waist he pulled her in closer, while his lips were sweet and soft against hers, he was happy, feeling better and he wanted to share that with her. Sitting naked in the soothing water to the sound of bubbles gurgling around his lean body, she watched them bounce off the strong muscled arms and was drawn to how gorgeous and sexy he looked.

Smiling she commented that, "Christmas is only a couple of weeks away, I should be out shopping and not lazing away beside you in luxurious bubbly water."

"Yeah you could be, but no one else is more important than us and we'll sort Christmas, in fact," he paused. "Let's have Friday together, you make a list of people and what presents we need to buy and we'll shop together so I don't have to let you go. We could have lunch out and back here with pizza and wine Friday night. What do you think?"

"Okay, I'll make a list later at home and we can make a day of it, that'll be fun."

"We're going to enjoy life together, and I'm happy for you to go home anytime you want," he reminded her smiling.

After rinsing the plates and stacking the dishwasher from the delicious roast vegetables and pork chops, they both blobbed out on the sofa so full that any thoughts of playfulness in the bedroom, would have to wait. Quiet contentment infused the entire room as they sat silently with Jonah's arm around the back of her now relaxed shoulders. Looking up into his sleepy eyes he smiled down at Gemma sending goose bumps racing erotically around her pale frame. Resting, they decide to watch a short programme on television before having an early night, after such an emotional day confronting the highs of life getting back to normal, still dealing with the unknown daunting lows that hung over them was emotionally exhausting.

In bed the crisp purple sheets cast a mood of romance as bodies lay close to each other, silently looking into his magical eyes and seeing the unguarded emotion. He had a twinkle in his eye, and they both knew how much in love they were.

Jonah put his home and farm on the market and there was a lot of interest, as land was always sort after. Especially good fertile land that could be used for horticulture. He began to sort out the things he no longer used and also the farm machinery that he no longer wanted, relying more on contractors instead of doing the work himself. Since hitting his head he had realized what he truly wanted in life. Jonah invited Gemma to an early Friday morning bacon and egg breakfast, he wanted to cook as he had insisted on the Christmas shopping day together, a fun day out with all the shopping done in one foul sweep. The list of names with suggestions of things to look out for was tucked in Gemma's handbag so that should help get through the shopping quicker.

Violet, (Jonah's mum) didn't know what she wanted for Christmas when Jonah asked her, apparently she only ever asks for money, but they decided to surprise her with a nice new fridge/freezer. She really needed more freezer space now, to have prepared meals ready frozen for her to microwave every day. Gemma would buy Jonah's present later on her own, so it would be a surprise for him.

The two of them were just cleaning up the dishes when the phone rang, it was Penelope, Jonah's real-estate agent. Jonah listened while she explained to him that the vender that he is buying the house from in February has found a home they want and wondered if they could bring the settlement forward to January.

"Yes," Jonah leapt at the opportunity, "I already have a lot of interest in my property and can put it to a January auction. Worst case scenario even if it doesn't sell, bridging finance is always an option. But it looks like it will. Can you arrange to change settlement date to January for me to buy the house so they can move on, no problem." Gemma heard him say.

Returning the phone to its cradle, Jonah looked at Gemma and reached for a cuddle, explaining that he was happy to go to auction because of the number of interested people who have already been through the farm.

"Oh, that's exciting I might be in our home right after getting married," Gemma exclaimed.

"Yes, and I'll get settled there before you move in." He smiled.

Christmas was nice although it came and went with little fuss as wedding and auction plans consumed all of their attention. Jonah was looking and feeling well with no headaches and they have put any doubts away and look forward to a wonderful future together. Jonah and Gemma now live life with as much time spent together as possible, his warm embrace and masculine cologne screaming out for attention, she found both provocative and stirring when he was near her and often caused her skin to tingle like an electric shock sizzling through her.

They were so attracted to each other and avoided any sleep overs now as married life drew closer. Staying away from each other had become more challenging as their love grew deeper every day and the self-control was like watching the sunrise taking forever to travel high in the sky. Gemma was counting down the days until she could live with this man for the rest of her life.

It wasn't long before auction day rolled around, it was being held in Jonah's home as his entire house and land package went up for sale. They were both seated comfortably together on the sofa in his office, listening intently with the door a little ajar so they could hear whispers as the tension spread thickly around the living room.

Although Jonah never displayed his emotions, Gemma knew he would obviously want to get an offer that would validate the time and effort he had spent. Gemma could feel the stress in the office, and his sentimental attachment as to what his farm was worth before moving on to a new home for them, with a jetty to accommodate the boat he already owned. The heavy presence of what was to come, will it sell? and the unnerving concern of, for how much? weighted them down. Gemma felt the pressure of his hand on hers, as they sat beside each other, there was nothing to say, the air was thick with tension and they just had to wait, listen and see. Gemma smiled and popped a kiss on his cheek, symbolizing that she understood. It must be hard to leave his farm he had built up over 30 years, fenced and cared for.

His forehead wrinkled tightly as they hear the first bid followed by a female voice bid, then back to two male voices, one gruff voice and then an assertive one topping that. The bidding war continued until the price went over two million. Gemma both nervous and excited all at once, people were competing for the estate. Her hand was squeezed quite firmly as Jonah eyed her with a smile, this was a positive sign, two buyers fighting over it and the price went up as did the excitement. Jonah was already happy nodding approval, but the bidding didn't stop. His eyes widened and tears welled in Gemma's eyes, excitement and disbelief as a cocktail of emotional relief and joy for Jonah flooded through her. She rested her head on his shoulder, wiping the happy tears away knowing that everything was going well. Jonah would be content to leave now with no regrets, his hard work had been rewarded, he'll be able to retire and go fishing with ample money in the bank. The hammer fell at 6.1 million, they both leapt up and faced each other, his eyes shining with a glint of moisture his mood one of elation, as his bright smile lit up his quiet demeanour. Satisfaction, speechless he looked down at her, positioned his arms around her waist and pulled her close into his body as his soft lips encircled hers and his tongue searched in her mouth.

"How are we going to celebrate tonight?" he finally found the strength to ask. "Shall we go somewhere nice for tea?" he laughed and swung Gemma off her feet.

Laughing, "Be careful, you'll hurt yourself."

The agent appeared smiling at the office door, tightly gripping the papers in her hand. Jonah signed acceptance.

"I don't think I can go home tonight, I'm too excited Jonah."

Settlement was in a couple of weeks and their new home would be empty next week, so they can move straight into it. It's all worked out really well." She managed to stammer, the excitement and disbelief making her a bit shaky, it was all so amazing, praise God.

"Our new home will be organised ready for me to move into after the wedding in February, I can even start packing some things to take." Her mind was a whirlpool of disbelief.

"There are only a few pieces of furniture to move, because I'll leave most at the cottage for us to stay overnight sometimes for a holiday at the beach."

"I know one day you'll get used to our new home together and feel no need for the cottage. We'll have a peaceful life together," he assured her nodding.

"Let's have a cup of tea, I need one after that, it has been extremely stressful and successful all at the same time," Gemma declared seizing a breath of air. They kept hugging each other, this was a life changing event.

"I'll head off, congratulations in your sale," said the jubilant real-estate agent. Pleased, she was looking forward to a winning commission coming her way.

"Our new home is quite lovely, but it needs fencing around the back yard for Wilson, it's good that you can have the moving truck pack and move you there next week, leaving the farm empty for the new owner the following week." Gemma said.

"Yes, it will be an easy move, I'll get the movers in to do everything, and you can help me sort our new home before the wedding." He smiled, walking her to the door.

"I can start packing your clothes from the wardrobe and box up the kitchen things ready for the moving men, I don't want any glassware to get broken." Her mind was racing in anticipation and organisation to be done.

"Come here you!" Jonah closed the gap between them, gently pulling her into his arms. "It feels so good that we can be financially secure and finally retired." A sigh of relief escaped his lungs now that it was all falling into place.

Every morning she took Wilson and drove to Jonah's to help pack; they were ready when the big day arrived. The moving truck pulled up and three men got out, they took the whiteware first, then the heavy furniture was strapped along the interior of the truck before proceeding to fill every space with the many boxes she had prepared.

Jonah's Ute was also fully laden and his car was chock-a-block. He drove to No.8 Amber Place anxious to supervise the men as they moved from room to room, then they give him a ride back to pick up his car. While they were away Gemma cleaned each empty room, there was not much to do as she had cleaned out all the kitchen cupboards as she emptied them.

Finally arriving back at the farm and the last truck load gone, Jonah followed with his carload and arranged for a ride back to meet up with her, he planned to spend a night at the cottage with Gemma.

When Jonah returned the house had been vacuumed and cleaned ready for the new owners. He looked tired and was as pale as a laid back albino cat. They were both exhausted after a busy day.

Reaching up to put her arms around his neck, "Its fish and chips tonight eh?"

"I think it's lucky we can go to yours, I don't feel like driving a third time today." He sighed as she lent into his chest.

"I have a thermos of tea made, and it's still light enough to go for a last walk around the property to say goodbye. I've fed Shed Cat and we can pick it up in the morning on your way, because he won't like Wilson at my home tonight," she suggested.

"He likes to be left alone, I hope he'll be happy living in the boat shed away from Wilson, once the fencing is up. I'll have to phone someone to put that up for us." He sounded very tired.

"Don't worry just relax and enjoy a last walk, you've done enough today. Everything is getting sorted and there are two of us now, you're not on your own to get unpacked." Giving his hand a reassuring squeeze. She and Wilson were okey at the cottage for now.

The last of the day's sun was setting in the sky, it had been a beautiful day and perfect weather, just hot work.

"You have a lot of unpacking to do now, but I'll give you a hand, I just can't stay over until Wilson can come too. I'm praying that this will be the last time either of us will ever move again." Gemma smiled up at Jonah as they hugged.

They started the long walk hand in hand down memory lane, along the dry cracked race that they had both walked many times, the one that he put a bulldozer through many years ago to create his life as a farmer. Along the same race where Gemma found him with a cut head and concussion. The lush paddocks now sat empty; all the animals had gone to the works so they didn't have to say goodbye to livestock. If she had to look at the beautiful animals, she would be saddened about saying goodbye to this glorious place.

Reminiscing Jonah spoke solemnly about his feelings, "I'm glad that the new owners want to keep the paddocks for stock, because it's good pasture, they have a good life roaming in the sunshine," he said reminiscing.

"You did well and now it's time to rest darling."

"Knowing my time for working in all sorts of weather is over and to have a change, to be free to do recreational fishing will be good." His head nodding in agreement.

Gemma attempted to lighten the moment as it was intense and serious as they walked hand in hand. "Do you remember my first winter walking down here with all the deep slush?" she asked him.

He burst out laughing, "I'll never forget that. You said, '*I don't want to know what I'm walking in!*' As you carefully tried not to fall over, your gumboot was sinking deep in cow shit that was sucking onto your boot every time you lifted your foot," he burst into hysterics again. "You were afraid of falling in with your lovely new jeans and red band gumboots on. That memory will always make me laugh," he said as he tucked her into his side for a loving cuddle. "You were never the farming type were you?"

Chapter 10

She laughed while making an excuse, "But I tried to help, I was brave. We will take our memories with us and make a lot more."

Reaching the orchard was bleaker, to think they planted it together and now they were leaving.

"It's nice that the fruit trees will keep growing long after we've gone, someone will benefit from the food that we planted." She smiled reassuringly.

"Yes, just as we are going to enjoy our new already grown orchard, so we won't miss out. We might still need to add some thornless berry fruit though, we enjoyed them." He smiled back.

"We will, we'll make it our own place."

The mood was tranquil and melancholy, as he pulled the front door closed for the last time on the grandeur that first confronted her when she came here to Jonah's farmhouse. Gemma's eyes blurry from fatigue, her mind was fixated on cheering Jonah. It will be a massive change for him.

The two of them silently, respectfully proceeded to drive to the cottage where Jonah received a doggy welcome of cheerful exuberance and full on wagging tail.

"Are you feeling up to a walk to the café for fish and chips or shall I go in the car and get some to have here at home?" she asked empathetically.

"Would you mind fetching tea as I don't feel I can do anymore today, I'm shattered," says Jonah.

"You put your feet up in front of television and I won't be long."

She fetched her purse from the bedroom and carefully reversed the car out of the garage feeling sorry for him, he looked physically exhausted and positive all at the same time. A couple of minutes drive found her standing alongside the sea wall, seabirds squawking as they circled overhead, a fishing boat had been gutting fish offshore and the birds fought for the pickings thrown overboard. The fisherman must have gotten back late, as they usually throw guts out in the channel to avoid stinky rubbish coming ashore, perhaps he thought he would miss the tide and not be able to get back in time.

Placing the order for two fish and chips to take away was convenient and they both really enjoyed the freshness of it for a quick tea, an early to bed night and waking up feeling refreshed ready to face another day tomorrow would be welcomed by them both.

Moving and settling in was tiring, but they eventually got through it, even though at times they thought they never would. Slowly possessions were finding a place and the house was getting tidier. Jonah's furniture, beds and unpacked clothes were hung in the wardrobe, it was taking shape and he would soon have all of his things in familiar drawers again. Not being able to stay with him tugged at her heart strings every time she left him in a strange house on his own, and Shed Cat was settling in as Jonah fed it in the boat house. Wilson and Gemma still couldn't stay yet, as distressing as it was because he would want to chase the cat. Jonah phoned the fencer and he would start to drill the post holes next week.

"What sort of fence should we have across the back yard?" Gemma asked while resting in Jonah's lounge, looking out to sea through floor to ceiling glass bi-fold doors.

"What about wrought iron so we can see through and it'll be in keeping with the character home," Jonah looked up from his book.

"Actually that would suit the house and make a wonderful place to grow old fashioned roses. A black fence with a pattern along the top, what do you think?" Heading over to her computer she tapped away bringing up styles online.

"Good idea, it will soon feel like home," he said.

Time now to focus on the extravagant affair, Jonah wanted their wedding to go perfectly, just like a dream come true. They had planned to have the reception at the farm but it will be more sentimentally appropriate to have the marquee erected at their new home.

By February No. 8 should be looking magnificent, with the reception held in a clearing amidst established fruit trees, the path to the orchard will be alive with colourful rows of hydrangea all looking their best in various shades of blue, lavender and pink with Gemma planning new planting additions of limelight hydrangea bushes scattered through on each side of the path, putting a personal touch of elegance to the garden. The giant central Magnolia at the front of the house with its empty circular garden will have a massive planting of flowers under it, they still have time to set an unforgettable aesthetically pleasing scene of scented delight for a beautiful outdoor reception.

Speaking on the phone with the very kind Reverend Fontaine, minister of the little country church they have booked to get married in, Gemma reassured him it was still happening, they wanted to get married in that church, even though they had moved house.

Jonah arranged to hire a bus to transport the guests from the church carpark in the morning and travel the half hour to the Waterworth bays area returning late in the afternoon following the reception. How amazing and wonderful to entertain and share their new home with all their friends, creating memories to not leave behind at the old farm.

The immediate thing to do now was to get the plants in the ground around the Magnolia tree and put sprinklers on them to help them get growing. Tuesday was a cool optimistic morning as she prepared to have an inspiring day out at the garden centre. Getting dressed in jeans and her favourite pink floral shirt; Jonah insisting on them having a nice lunch at the garden café and Gemma was anticipating a lovely day together.

Strolling around a garden centre was perfect therapy to relax and unwind ready for the excitement of the upcoming wedding, so much had happened, leaving the farm and its lifestyle was emotionally arduous and getting settled into the new home physically challenging and time consuming. The fencing has now been erected and Jonah's elated to finally house his boat, moored in the boat house out of the weather and it was now on the doorstep, available to use whenever the mood takes him, it was a fantastic incentive to retire and live life at a slower pace. In the past, it had been annoying to have to specify a time to go fishing, fitting it in around the cattle and stringent feeding out of silage. Now, he could go whenever the tide was right, that spurred him on and he really looked forward to some leisurely time.

The limelight hydrangeas were pre-ordered online to insure she has the eight plants needed. They were both able to leisurely stroll around the garden centre and take time to browse and discuss the many beautiful plants, all showing promise of new growth.

Jonah filled the shopping trolley with four thornless boysenberry bushes, also purchasing large clumps of cream coloured day lilies to circle the deep wine coloured magnolia tree, they would have an abundance of flowers opening right through summer. As they chatted Gemma suggested ground cover geraniums to spread around the rest of the garden in a variety adorned with masses of cream edged pink flowers which promised to spread rapidly to cover the garden bed. Jonah and Gemma enjoyed a glorious day at the garden centre, so after collecting the ordered hydrangeas and positioning them into Jonah's Ute, they headed back indoors to the centre café for a nice frothy coffee and some lunch.

The weekend would be spent planting and adding bags of fertilizer enriched compost, to give them all the best possible start.

Late on Sunday Gemma returned to the beach cottage where they carefully packed her special pieces of furniture onto the Ute and drove back to Waterworth in preparation for her to move in later, only leaving behind a small, very basic chest of drawers to use in the meantime until the wedding. Seeing her familiar possessions spread around No. 8 Amber Place was bizarre and uncomfortable as although the move was composed and orderly her insides were a whirlwind.

Gemma was cautiously elated to close one chapter of her life, nervous and excited to start another full of hope and anticipation of bringing the serenity of the cottage with her to their new home.

So much had happened in just a short space of time, meeting Jonah, wedding plans and purchasing an unbelievably beautiful new home, it was difficult to comprehend how he drew her out of her reclusive sanctuary to share a new life with him in just a few short years. The once upon a time curtain of doubt and darkness had begun to be drawn. Gemma's heart had let a little hope shine through, she was too busy experiencing their everyday together, not wanting to waste a moment of these precious years, they were so fortunate to have been granted together.

With the new fences in place Gemma sporadically stayed over and Wilson was confined to the yard and could not get to 'Shed Cat' who settled in and loved life in the old, weathered boathouse pouncing on the odd water rat.

Jonah and she were exuberant and like a new day dawning, the wedding day couldn't come soon enough. Invitations had gone out explaining that transport from the church to reception was arranged and acceptance replies came rushing into Jonah's letterbox.

Opening her emails, there was a message from Gemma's eldest brother Stanley which read, he and her other brother Len would fly over from Australia to be at the wedding, their wives cannot make it, but they are able to stay for a few days. Oh, her stomach was a flutter of butterflies and her head was sky high in a fog, she was so thrilled. How wonderful that her brothers will make the trip to be at the wedding. Gemma promptly pushed 'Reply' and typed a message.

"That's wonderful news, you can stay in my cottage and use my little car to get to the church service, you can either leave the car at the church or drive to be with Jonah at the house when I'm getting ready for the wedding. But either way you don't have to worry about accommodation as the cottage has three bedrooms. I look forward to seeing you both." Thrilled to have her brothers at her wedding she pushed Send! and logged off.

Grabbing for the landline phone, unable to wait until 7pm to give Jonah the good news she hastened to push his number.

"My brothers will be coming to our wedding," Gemma yelled excitedly down the phone she held tightly in her hand, her bare feet bouncing up and down on the soft carpet as she was unable to stay still.

"That's lovely sweetheart, it'll be nice to have your family here," he said. Gemma could picture his sincere smile from the sound of his voice.

They were both cheerful and full of energy in anticipation of not only getting married but also catching up with family and friends they had neglected of late, and Gemma was pleased for Jonah that his sister will collect his mum to bring as well.

Because of Violets age she would be unable to stay long at the reception, however it was good that she was making time to meet everyone and see how beautiful the marque and flowers were. Gemma was grateful for her presence as an acknowledgement of them getting married.

Now in their late sixties neither Gemma nor Jonah had a lot of family left, so it will be lovely to have them present at the wedding. Although the day would be about the commitment they wanted to make to each other, they will also enjoy sharing their special day and catching up with the many friends they have, some of whom have not had the chance to know them as a couple.

Jonah has family in Australia who can not get to New Zealand in time for the wedding, so later on after the wedding day the happy couple plan to travel around for their honeymoon, including a visit to everyone who could not make it on the day. They were happy to keep the wedding small and intimate, and with plans for the honeymoon to be in Australia, which would allow them a short time to meet those they needed to, after some initial touring around together. They had allowed 10 days before flying back home to New Zealand.

"As long as we're together," Gemma said. "Honestly I'm happy wherever we go to meet them all." Knowing, after which time they would head home to enjoy the rest of their lives in their Waterworth Bays home alone with Wilson and the boat house cat that Bridget was feeding.

An unbelievably glorious Saturday morning, the 22nd of February 2021 ultimately arrived and her daughter Bridget was with her to help calm her nerves and prepare. Gemma was so excited as they hastily had breakfast together, home in the cottage. The anxiety making it difficult for Gemma to sit still for long. There was a knock on the door, startled and on edge she leapt up. Opening the door to a courier man who presented her with a box which had a translucent lid, an undeniably beautiful bouquet sat nestled inside, soft pink and cream roses arranged with white sweet peas all of which created a glorious fragrance, even in the box. It was just like a dream come true. What a brilliant florist to make her wish come true, the scent was incredible and Gemma was very pleased.

Everything was going well, up popped a text message from Jonah to say he had his suit and tie already lying on the bed and he can't wait to see her down the aisle, his beautiful bride. Texting for her not to worry everything was under control.

The weather was an unnecessary concern as February had brought them a beautiful calm day, and the marquee was erected without any problems down one end of the orchard looking incredible. The florist has worked her magic on all of the tables, creating stunning arrangements on each one.

Bridget reported to Gemma that she has been to check and had draped the backs of the white chairs in the marque with large bows of royal blue ribbons, the same colour as the guys were wearing in their ties with grey suits. Promising her mum that everything was under control and for Gemma to only worry about looking lovely. The dressmaker had also done a brilliant job of the dresses and they were both hanging in the wardrobe with the door ajar, so Gemma could keep looking at them, unable to believe this was really happening, she was getting married. Bridget suggested that they have a slow walk to the beach as the weather was calm and it would help to fill in the time before this afternoons wedding. Gemma agreed as she didn't know what to do with herself, and although not gone long but it was therapeutic. Relaxed, and after having yet another cup of tea they decided to have a light lunch before it was time to get dressed and carefully apply their makeup.

Gemma had decided she did not want a hairdresser today as the highlights and colour had been done last week, it didn't need cutting as she wanted to leave her hair long. Gemma's eyes sparkled when she saw how beautiful Bridget looked in her dress, the blue complementing her azure eyes.

Bridget beamed with delight looking into the mirror and commented how much fun it was to be able to go to her mother's wedding. She fussed around Gemma getting ready and informed her when it was time to go, the bridal car had arrived. The last thing to do, Bridget helped to attach her mum's short veil to a tulle daisy head piece on top of her long loose hair, teasing the veil like a cloud around her shoulders. The two ladies stood in front of the mirror, it was done, they looked lovely, Gemma gently picked up her beautiful bouquet, the time had come for Gemma to get married.

A shiny black limousine with white ribbons shimmering along the hood was waiting patiently to pick them up from the cottage and take them to the quant country church, Jonah insisted on them travelling in style today. He had also hired a photographer, a tall lanky guy of a responsible age who would record photos of the day to look back on in years to come.

Gemma stepped out of the front door, resplendent in white, Bridget pulled it closed behind her. She was pleasantly surprised to see the street was lined with a row of smiling neighbours who had come out to stand and wave, her heart swelled with how kind they were and how special today was. Lifting a hand she smiled and waved back just like royalty. The drive to the church was special, slow, sedate and calm as she enjoyed every moment.

The limousine turned safely into the church driveway and the driver got out, rushing around the car to help hold the door open as they alight from the back seats. Gemma took time to stand beside the rose garden to carefully brush her wedding gown down with her hands, insuring that it hung perfectly. Bridget was alert to her duty as she went to carefully peep through the arched church doorway. Her mum was ready and everything was in order, she signalled to the pianist to start playing the bridal march. Gemma's brother Stanley was waiting to one side of the double doors. Smartly dressed in a grey suit and royal blue tie, just like Jonah's groomsman Mike. Gemma spotted him straight away when she stepped through into the foyer and her face lit up.

"Oh, this is a surprise," she beamed at him, her heart warmed and he gave her a careful hug so as not to mess her dress up.

"Your lovely man asked that I give you away, if that's okay with you," he whispered.

"Oh yes, you look very nice. I was prepared to walk down the aisle on my own, but I would love for you to give me away. Thank you." She burst forth excited. Jonah had thought of everything, what a lovely surprise for his soon to be wife, to give her the perfect day.

The minister indicated for everyone to stand as the music started to fill the historic wooden interior. Gemma slowly made her way down the aisle, escorted on her brothers arm. The sweet perfume filled the air from the two massive floral arrangements standing tall on either side of Reverend Fontaine, and the whispered sound of awe could be heard from everyone lovingly watching as she drew closer to her destination. Jonah turned to smile, as he stood beside his long time friend Mike, they all waited for Gemma to do the slow walk to the beautiful sound of the piano. Bridget followed on slightly behind them after she had checked the back of the veil was still looking perfectly to her liking. Walking proudly with self-assurance and spirituality, a church wedding was so special, it was just what Gemma always imagined to be the right way to get married. She felt confident in her choice and happily walked to stand side by side with Jonah for the rest of their lives.

Back in the pews, faces turned to smile and whisper, she recognised friends and family who had come to witness this spectacular day in her life, a day that she once thought would never come again. Finally, standing beside him they said their vows, looking into each other's eyes.

"Who gives this woman in marriage?" asks Reverend Fontaine.

"I do," says Stanley loudly, before he was heard shuffling off to be seated over to the side. The church was so quiet; everyone was focused on the proceedings with only the click of a camera heard around the church. The ceremony continued, Gemma and Jonah said vows to each other, exchanging simple gold rings as they were pronounced husband and wife, awkwardly they kissed gently, unaccustomed to having an audience. They both bent to sign the document laid on a tiny round table and Gemma giggled shyly, before turning with cheerful faces to walk back down the aisle as husband and wife. Standing outside the church doorway, the camera started flashing as smiling faces greet, meet and thank their guests for coming. After which, the guests scrambled into the waiting chartered bus and bride and groom waved and said they would see everyone at the house for the reception.

Chapter 11

Arriving at the marquee guests exit from the bus to delicious looking drinks being passed around on silver trays. The two tiered royal iced wedding cake was observed and remarked upon as it stood with distinction on a separate circular table beside the bridle table.

The long bridle table was extravagantly adorned with masses of lilies and perfumed sweet peas, long green and white gypsophila cascading down the front of the crisp white tablecloth and the royal blue bows presenting a cooling special relaxed ambiance on this hot afternoon. At one end of the marquee a parquet floor had been laid down for dancing, with strings of tiny lights strung overhead. When the sun set and as the dusk settled they flickered delicate soft shadows around the marquee.

Everything looked magical and the guests were contentedly mingling, drinking cool cocktails and chatting while the happy couple sat in the house to gather themselves, sharing some time together before being seated at the long table for a catered wedding dinner. Jonah's starry eyes glistened with moisture with an emotional look that lovingly melted her heart.

They made their way to be seated for the meal, first getting over the necessary formality of thank you and welcome, everyone set about enjoying the meal courses with chatter, mingling and laughter. After which, Jonah stood and offered his hand to his bride for a dance and there was an instantaneous silence around the marque as they walked onto the floor. It seemed like the whole world was watching, as it became obvious to all that Jonah and Gemma both had a love for dancing, amidst applause the music ended as they went to sit down allowing the guests to have the floor for a short time, the temptation to dance was intense and as the DJ played outstanding dance music, Jonah and Gemma joined in for more dancing.

The whole evening went according to plan, it had been a festive day, the wedding was beautiful, emotional and joyous with the marquee being a perfect setting for the reception. As the evening drew to an end the happy couple stood to cut the cake, and the staff arranged for small silver coloured cake boxes of rich wedding cake to be arranged around the cake table, placed there for all of the guests to take with them as they departed to the bus which was waiting to return them to their cars.

After saying goodbye to them all as Mrs Frederick, her brothers Len and Stanley advised Gemma they would leave her car at the cottage as they have an airport shuttle picking them up tomorrow, to fly home to Brisbane, Australia. After everyone had left, Gemma and Jonah stood stunned inside their new home. Peace and quiet after all the excitement of the day, they took a deep breath as their new life began. Jonah poured two glasses of champagne to have a relaxing drink just the two of them.

"Wait a moment, I'll be back." She scurries off to the back door and let Wilson join them as they finally succumb to the tiredness brought on by an incredibly memorable day.

Alone and embracing each other, sharing the thrill of anticipation which could finally be quenched before falling asleep in a long awaited bliss.

Waking in the morning to the sound of the birds skimming the water for insects just down at the bottom of the yard was amazing, Gemma felt light and happy with a completeness never experienced before. Not rushing to get up, they spent time together before rising from bed, Jonah went to get them both breakfast while she jumped in the shower. Peacefully standing under the gentle spray of water showering down on her, Gemma was mindful of feeling so lucky and recalled the warmth in his eyes when he looks at her. Making love was incredible, just two people who were totally at ease with each other, she felt that the time spent getting to know each other as friends, years of kindness and patience had paid dividends.

She dressed and strolled outside to sit and take everything in, her new home, the fresh air, only to find the outdoor table laid out with cups of tea and toast and a selection of honey, jam and marmalade, her husband smiled from across the table.

Settling down opposite him she relaxed and watched Wilson, he was thriving on all the running around and exploring, definitely not missing his walks as now he had a bigger lawn. They laughed as they watched him, he had invented a new game, he liked jumping off the jetty and creating a loud splash as he landed in the water, before doggy paddling the short distance back to the grassed area, looking completely drowned, he headed back to do another jump, and it was quite comical. Looking further to the side she could see the marque still looking magnificent in the orchard, it would be packed up and gone before they return from Australia, and Bridget would take Wilson home with her, she planned to pick him up that afternoon. Wilson was very fond of Bridget and would jump into her car no problem.

Two suitcases sat packed and ready to fly to Australia later today and they would land in Sydney to meet relatives who did not come to New Zealand. It was a combination of responsibility, but also to meet Jonah's family. Jonah had booked a nice motel to stay in Adelaide for a few days and fly home via Sydney, so they will again stay in another lovely motel for one night allowing them to do some shopping before flying home. The airport shuttle bus had been ordered to collect them from home and take them to the airport so that their first day of married life would be slow and stress-free. Jonah was already dreaming of croissants and bacon for tomorrow's breakfast in the motel.

Hanging on the bedroom door handle were Gemma's sky-blue lightweight trousers and silk blouse to wear, Jonah liked her wearing blue to match her eyes. They were prepared for the temperature to be hot when they arrived in Adelaide so she had chosen cool fabrics.

The first time Jonah attempted to get his boat out of the boat house she was very tense, watching nervously knowing that it would be a new challenge that they both would need to get used to, Gemma was afraid in case the boat ran off the track or perhaps Jonah found it took more strength than he had. Fortunately, her fears were unfounded as gravity helped slide it down the two sloping metal runners with very little effort as it slid out of the shed beside the jetty and glided onto the water with ease. Standing on the lawn supervising, Gemma was pleased it all went effortlessly because the chain winch held the boat tightly, as Jonah cranked the lever round and round slowly allowing the boat to slide down the tracks and into the water. Then he just disconnected it from the boat and stepped off the floating jetty and onto the boat ready to start up the motor.

Gemma waved to him and breathed a sigh of relief as he proudly exhibited a sweeping confident grin across his face, he was living his dream.

Trudging back to the house through tall unmown grass, her feet warm and dry in her trusty gumboots with Wilson constantly beside her, what a wonderful companion as he sprawled out on the lawn beside Gemma and she began to do some gardening, starting with trimming off the spent flowers from the hydrangeas. Gemma always found time disappeared while happily toiling in the garden, soaking in the beauty of the flowers and feeling content in her work it was surprising how many hours she could wile away; when eventually getting a tired back she accepted that it was time to go back inside. With Wilson plonking himself at her feet while she relaxed over a cup of tea, she decided that these boat outings would provide a fantastic chance to catch up on some reading.

Removing the crochet bookmark she remembers making many years ago, she read the words cross-stitched on it, *'There's no place like home,'* she began to read and thought how true! After a while she looked up from the book, suitably rested in one of Jonah's comfortable old armchairs, the one that had a view of the jetty.

It did seem like quite a while that Jonah had been gone, she considered and looked forward to seeing him arrive home, she kept an eye out glancing up and down from her book keen to catch sight of him as he stepped off the boat, before going into the shed. The armchair was in a good spot to see him arrive home, and she was quick to look up and see him as he appeared with the chain in hand hooking the boat to the winch.

She kept still so as not to attract his attention through the glass window, she enjoyed watching his concentration from a distance and thoughtfully counted her blessings, she was so lucky to have this wonderful man in her life. Watching, he manages to haul up the boat as it slowly disappeared back into the boathouse prior to his walk back towards the house. Dropping his wet clothes on the back porch Jonah had not a care in the world, happily ignoring that he only had a T-shirt and underpants on as he walked over to see her. Bending and reaching his arms down towards Gemma he embraced her in a giant bear hug. He has had a good day.

"Come and have a look outside on the porch," he said smiling.

Replacing the bookmark between the pages Gemma stood up to follow him outside. Without speaking, Jonah picked up a bucket. Wilson was curious, watching as she peered into the smelly bucket with two shiny dead fish lying in it, their eyes were staring and they looked wet and scaly, Jonah seemed very pleased with himself.

"Umm, I don't know what to do with fish, my fish always come battered or crumbed out of a carton," she explained, a little stunned and reluctant to reach for the bucket being offered to her.

"Okay, I'll cook the fish from now on." He laughed, very pleased with himself.

The look of shock on Gemma's face was enough that he never asked her again, another wonderful memory for him to treasure, he grinned to himself. It was a month later, on a lovely sunny day he suggested they go out for a ride in the boat with his promise of no fishing.

"Okay I'm game," shouted Gemma with a smile, she should get involved in his new hobby.

"I think I should get a bigger motor for the boat really, as this little one isn't very powerful. It has seen better years but it'll do for now," he murmured.

"Will it be okay to go out with it today though?" she started to have doubts knowing that she wasn't great on water.

"Oh yes, for local fishing it'll be fine, I might just replace the old blade for a while," he said, thinking that he would get round to it one day.

Gemma found a day bobbing around on the ocean rather tedious, being stuck in a small area surrounded by water, it really wasn't her. However she didn't say that to Jonah, as he loved it. Not much was said as he eyed her, he saw her discomfort and has since been happy to make friends with other fisherman and leave her in the garden, which worked for them both. Gemma went out on bus trips with the garden club once a month and takes Wilson for walks around the neighbouring streets. They continued to enjoy dancing together with Jonah incorporating a lot of interesting moves, plus he liked to look for more online so it kept the dancing fresh and exciting.

Every Friday night they went to the local dance hall and had made a lot of wonderful friends, while continuing to share their love of dancing together. Dancing gave Gemma the excuse to pull off the rubber gardening gloves and buy new dresses, while Jonah put away the fishing gear, and they have an evening of getting all dressed up to meet up with friends, it was great fun. The community hall had a large dance floor, lots of tables and chairs to sit around and just watch if that was all someone wanted to do. That was where they met Lynda and Paul a nice couple in their late 70s. Sitting at the same table on a Friday evening everyone shared their news on how the family were getting on, their homes and any updates on new grandchildren. Married life was good.

Gemma sat listening to Lynda, she was interested in hearing about the rural holiday home Lynda and Paul own up north, she spoke enthusiastically about the renovating and building a big addition to it, one day to make it their permanent home. As soon as the addition was finished they intended to sell the suburban house they live in at present. Gemma listened attentively to the kitchen plans and what they wanted to do, they felt impatient to move because of the build-up of fast moving traffic and constant infill housing around their home. Finding it overwhelming, the increased number of people and cars now on the road compared to when they first built there thirty years ago, had become too much for them to cope with as they grew older.

Gemma and Jonah had felt the same, that was why they struggled to find their home and consider themselves very lucky to be in an old street with established big sections, homes that are hopefully loved by their owners who also enjoy privacy of a large section and trees. Plus, they still had the beach cottage for holidays to escape to. Gemma felt they would be missed when Lynda moved away as it will be too far for them to continue to come dancing each week, Paul wouldn't mind giving up dancing but Lynda will miss it terribly. It not only provided socializing opportunity but was also a fun way to exercise. They promised to keep in touch and visit when they make the move away.

Days grew into weeks and since moving to their home Gemma has made a conscious effort to chat and be sociable with the neighbours, she was thankful she made the decision to join the once a month gardening club. The group of ladies go on outings, giving her the opportunity to see all sorts of styles, providing her with a mound of ideas for her garden. Some of the outings were to private gardens in outlying areas that wouldn't normally be open to the public and she had enjoyed them.

"Jonah do you remember that I'm going out this Thursday with the gardening club?" She asked between sips of refreshing berry fruit tea.

"Umm yes, that'll be nice for you, this week is forecast to have brilliant weather so I'll spend the day out in the boat and perhaps have fish for tea." He smiled and glanced over his reading glasses; he knew that meant he gets to cook if he catches any fish.

Thursday arrived and she kissed and hugged him before driving herself to the pick-up point the club arranged, it provided easy parking so all the members could board the bus. The charter bus arrived early and they all got ticked off the list, Betty still hadn't arrived. Margaret pulled out her mobile and rang her number, sounding very efficient she reported back to everyone standing in the carpark that the missing person was just about there, they won't have long to wait. It was easy to chat with the ladies, even strangers because everyone was wearing club name tags and she felt confident enough to just go up and introduce herself.

Sunscreen was passed around and everyone had a sunhat in their handbags. The last person drove into the carpark and members excitedly clambered onto the bus for a seat, with a vociferous noise of ladies all talking at once, Margaret then stood up the front of the very nice coach to greet and introduce 'Max' an older driver before advising of the itinerary for the day. Everyone was relaxed and noisy as she settled into the fabric seat, adjusting the overhead conditioner ready for a nice day, it all seemed very well organized.

Anne, with snow white hair sat beside Gemma. "This is a different driver to the one we normally have," she whispered. Arousing a flicker of concern when the driver had several attempts to turn the bus around.

All chatter stopped; silence as someone whispered that perhaps he's just new to driving buses!

Departing the carpark he drove too close to the trees which lined the passenger side of the driveway, and as branches brushed along the coach windows, the painful cracking of branches could also be heard scrapping and breaking off. There was a cloak of silence as they all held their breath and an unease seemed to blow from the air conditioner as nothing was said and everyone sat anxiously waiting.

Max, then displaying a hesitancy himself, decided to check with Margaret which way to go and she provided directions, before taking her seat. Driving along the highway everyone settled down once more, until she pointed out to the driver that he should be in the left lane because we need to take the next turn-off. Difficulty averted thank goodness for Margaret, or who knows where they might have ended up.

First stop was a lovely red painted café with a nice outdoor seating area and they were ready for their arrival, with a prepared morning tea, scrumptious savouries and slices and the coffee was very welcoming now at 10.30am. Most of the members chose to sit at the outdoor tables covered with plastic floral tablecloths, which was acceptable, being practical. Looking around at the variety of members sun hats was interesting, some were plan and sensible, some had comical characters or comments and others were bright florals suitably welcoming of the occasion. Gemma giggled, making herself a mental note of how the hats often reflected the type of person wearing them. Climbing back into the coach, which was thankfully parked in the shade they all headed off to view the first country garden.

This garden was a business venue for weddings and special events, its main feature being a beautiful large pond covered with tall purple flowering water lilies and with a simple flat lawn beside it. The unique brick archway appeared to be hand crafted by the owner or someone creative, it was apparently used for the bride and groom to stand under to have wedding photos taken, it had a rustic look, picturesque with a splattering of ivy growing over it. Strolling around this garden failed to inspire Gemma, as she always searched out flowers, and to her this garden had a lot of interesting features but was lacking in enough flowers, its formal design was very professional and it had a lovely restaurant attached for functions to be held indoors. Flowers were her interest, and she liked to see what and where people planted them, the colour combinations that people choose, and her expectation was that the next garden would be more her.

Arriving at a private home that they open by appointment only, they drove into a no exit street and again the coach had difficulty, turning to park was challenging enough without the open drains on either side of a gravel road. Margaret got out to help direct the driver so he didn't reverse the bus into the gutter. After some time carefully manoeuvring everyone could finally relax and disembark.

Welcomed by the owner who introduced himself as Oliver, a tall gentleman wearing a cream hat over very bushy white eyebrows, and the beautiful homestead called 'Lucas House'. Nicely spoken and very English like, he explained that they had lunch prepared for everyone later after wandering around viewing the grounds, the advice was to take a seat at the outdoor tables after the finished tour or if it was decided enough walking had been done around the two hectare property; he gestured towards the grand white house towering over the lawn with layers of curved steps looking down onto the stream, and pointed off to the left-hand side where an ample number of clean white tables and white wooden chairs for all to relax in were located.

Strolling around the garden, the club members unintentionally formed into small groups of ladies who discussed various plants and flowers that they prefer, the aromatic herb garden was of interest to some and the oldie world roses with their intoxicating beauty to

Gemma and the ladies around her, repeatedly bent over smelling the various sweet scents and enjoying colours while comparing the many varieties and shapes, some of which were familiar, especially the hybrid tea roses such as her favourite 'Aotearoa' which is an elegant pink with an outstanding perfume and the ladies all discussed rose names and exchanged information, what a gorgeous place. After all the admiring and complements of how beautiful everything was the day was capped off by the host providing them with a delicious lunch, all served on genuine old English china with floral cups and saucers, an array of club sandwiches and small dainty triangles of soft bread covered with cheese and pickle. The three tiered china cake stands were laden with tiny butterfly cakes and a variety of slices, scattered strawberries and pineapple pieces placed around the edges was charming and well presented in this exquisite setting.

    Relaxing in tranquil ambiance looking around the lawn they gathered, sheltering from the hot sun under cool umbrellas and all 53 members finished a wonderful lunch. Unrushed they were invited to enjoy walking the spectacular board walk around the meandering stream, lined with ferns and purple iris, before strolling in the shade of the many old weeping willow trees where a couple of concrete sheep were spotted laying on the lawn, so lifelike, no one could resist taking a photo of them. With heartfelt thanks they all said goodbye and the hum of happy chatter could be heard as they took a seat back on the coach to head home, a very satisfying day had by all of the retired ladies and one gent, now tired from heat, eating too much and walking further than one would normally do. The drive back to the carpark to collect private cars went without a hitch, there was little traffic on the road and Max's nervous start has diminished. He had relaxed and enjoyed the day as much as all the members and hopefully he had made friends as well.

    Arriving home, Jonah has a bucket of fish covered on the back porch, he also had a successful day and Gemma was pleased as she wouldn't be cooking tea tonight.

Back she went to the kitchen she put the jug on for a cuppa in time to share today's events with each other. The days that follow her garden trips out were spent with renewed enthusiasm in her own garden now inspired by the lovely places she had seen. Standing in front of her own wooden archway erected over a long wooden seat, which she painted white and planted scented Star Jasmine to cover it she observed and acknowledged how fast it had grown and established itself quickly with the March heat and lots of watering every week. It wouldn't be long before the archway provided romance and shade for their home, she was content with her life.

While Gemma gains pleasure from watching things grow, Jonah had been building friendships with others out on their boats as he chatted with newfound fishing mates about whatever men talk about. Stephan introduced himself, he was one guy in particular who they see a lot of, as he had become a good fishing buddy for Jonah. Conveniently living just five minutes down the road he met Jonah out on the water when they dropped anchor under seagulls as they circled an area, both men ended up fishing in the same spot while throwing a can of beer across to each other. Stephan will sometimes moor his boat in Jonahs jetty and they both came up to the house for a cold beer on a hot day or a hot coffee to perk them up.

Stephan was polite, retired and married, a wife at home who didn't care much for sitting on a boat in glaring hot sunshine. Occasionally, Jonah took Wilson on *'Jonah's Gem'* for a couple of hours, carefully lifting him into the boat, their loyal ageing dog appeared to almost smile as he lay down on the wooden slat flooring soaking in the warmth of the sun, watching seagulls hover overhead, growing older but still having that sense of duty and responsibility of now looking after both of them.

Over the years Gemma and Jonah have lost count of how many times Jonah derived enjoyment from being out on the rolling tide, each time appearing like he came back renewed and sometimes with a proud smile and a bucket of fish that Gemma avoided.

Gemma could relate to feeling that way, she remembers breathing in the sea-air and letting worries float away when she lived at Latent beach and needed to retreat into her own thoughts. She still visited the cottage to spend time toiling away the hours in her cottage garden and walking on the beach, she holds dear the tranquil peace gained and was sure those fond memories would always be with her.

Chapter 12

The cottage by the sea had become their holiday home and sometimes they spent lazy weekends there together; the house now seemed small and paltry compared to their big home with its character features of fretwork and wooden trim. The happy couple continued on their journey to enjoy their new home, decorating it to blend more gently into the environment by having the harsh white repainted to a softer lime white, now easier on the eye and mentally bringing a peaceful tranquillity to it. Gemma's joy of planting hundreds of daffodils up the driveway as she once dreamed of, has come to fruition. Every July she anxiously waited, it was always exciting to see them multiply and bloom come spring, they both held their breath in anticipation of a spectacular show year after year and were never disappointed.

Relaxing at her writing desk and checking out emails, she reads about the forthcoming trip and called out to Jonah.

"Jonah, this month's outing with the gardening club is visiting a lavender garden, it's a bus trip with a stop for morning tea on the way. We're going to a private home up Wellsford way, do you feel like a day out? Shall I put us both down for a seat?" she inquired.

"No, not this time thanks, you have a nice chat with your lady friends and I'll catch up with Stephan for a beer."

"Are you sure? I'll be gone all day, and they do sell lavender products at the craft shop on the property if you're interested."

"No, it's not my thing, but if you see anything nice then you buy it, lavender soap is always good in the bathroom and don't forget to put a gift in the cupboard to keep for someone later," he suggested.

"Okay, you'll probably enjoy a get together with Stephan, invite a few guys around if you want. Get in some beer and I'll get some sausage rolls for you all," she promised.

"What day is it planned for?" Walking over to check the calendar hanging on the wall.

"Thursday 20th October, a week away," she advised him.

"Put some sausage rolls in the freezer in case I have anyone come around, they won't go to waste," he murmured while deep in thought.

"Okay, next shopping day." Gemma made a mental note to add it to her shopping list.

They were both pleased with the decision to buy here. They had a social life independent of each other and continue to enjoy dancing together. Everyday was driven to form another month, growing towards another year gone by, and without noticing it, Gemma and Jonah had been favoured with nine wonderful years of married life. Life was kind to them and as the crinkles and wrinkles appeared along with grey hair they enjoyed hobbies, interests and friends. Gemma constantly enjoying her forever changing garden.

'Jonah's Gem' was often at sea and there was always that proud smile when he brought home fresh fish for tea. It frequently surprised Gemma that her heart melted and did a flip every time his boat arrived back at the bottom of the property, she awaits his return from sea and one of the things she loved about him was when she was cooking tea, now and again he would play his guitar and sing. The sound so delightful it sent little trills to her heart, propitious reminders of being with him. When he starts to sing, she can't resist turning the stove elements down to simmer the food, it continued cooking while she joined him in song, just the two of them ecstatic about each other and everything they do together. Year after year, life continued to be wonderful, he listened and supported her pursuits in the garden and he inspired her to keep writing now she had taken that up. Jonah was enthusiastic, taking an interest in her

stories, proof reading and commenting. Gemma smiled and listened to his suggestions feeling blessed.

Waking up one bitter cold July morning looking out to sea, the high tide of the water was creeping its way around the property and gushing hungrily under the jetty, further out the sea was heaving huge waves up into the air, and with a deafening boom against the wooden railings they receded back into a cold angry sea, like a furious whale complaining and landing with a thud. Jonah lit the fire in the lounge for them to stay warm as Gemma finished up the breakfast dishes in the kitchen.

"It's a bit rough on the water, but I feel like taking the boat out, just for a short time. It's hard to stay indoors now that I'm used to free time to do whatever I want," he laughed.

"Oh, are you sure you should do that? The sea looks wild today and it's only early; it might get worse, we're in July now," warned Gemma with concerned panic evident in her voice.

"I'm so used to our little bit of the world now, that I'm not worried, there are dark clouds on the horizon but I know my way around, and the fish might be biting," he insisted.

"I think the fish will have more sense and be hiding deep down below the waves," expressing her concern, she really was uneasy about his plan.

"The weather forecast says rough weather is on the way, but the sea is right here at the door. I won't go far out and I'll just go out quickly and be back before any storm hits. Which could be hours away, you know what the forecasts are like," he protested.

Reluctantly against her better judgement she agreed, "Okay, don't be long, what time will you be back?"

"I'll probably only be gone about 2 hours, all going well. If it worsens I'll turn back, promise," he says.

She could not understand his decision and so again attempted to change his mind.

"Can't you stay home and enjoy the fire; we can watch a movie?" she suggested with a hint of pleading in her voice.

Laughing it off, "No, don't worry there's no problem." He smiled undeterred.

The turmoil inside Gemma's stomach was equal to the ocean. She questioned if he had possibly become overly confident, not respecting the sea and she was not happy about his decision to go, however, not wanting to cause a problem if he was determined. She understood the frustration of staying inside after connecting with nature the way they both have. Gemma had often run out into the rain to tie up a tree or save a plant.

While Jonah made haste to get the fishing tackle and warm clothes, she made him a thermos flash of coffee, then dragged out her cookery books from under the cold marble benchtop to consider what to bake. She figured that baking would kill two birds with one stone, keeping her warm with the oven on, and having nice treats for him when he got back. Hopefully, with the bonus of reducing her concerns of him being out in the cold. Thumbing through her familiar old recipes, she settled on chocolate chip biscuits and set about gathering the trays, large bowl and mixing spoon while lining up the ingredients along the top of the bench, mindfully occupied mumbling, 'Two eggs, No! I have a dozen so may as well make a double batch and have plenty of biscuits for the freezer. Four eggs, flour, sugar, butter, baking powder and a large, lidded container that was nearly full of chunky chocolate bits, yum.'

"I'm off love see you later," he called out, quickly returning to pop a gentle kiss on her check, side on to him as she turned the oven up to 180c.

"Bye don't worry if you don't catch anything, just get back before the storm comes our way. Don't forget your flask of coffee." Pointing in the flask direction with an outstretched arm.

"Will do," he laughed, carefree while heavily clad in all his wet weather gear.

Looking at the large round clock on the kitchen wall it was only 10am, she planned to have a good lot of chocolate chippies by lunch time when he was due back, her eyes pursue him through the kitchen window and she paused to watch as he walked down the lawn buckling up his lifejacket on the way, he looked back at the kitchen window and she blew him a kiss before he turned into the boat house.

She tried to focus and get on with it, choosing to relax by listening to music while baking, she wandered over to turn on the radio channel. The melodies burst forth breaking the silence with sounds from the 60s, and Rock n Roll cheered her work in the warm kitchen. Wilson looked up in disgust from his wannabe sleep as she accidently clanged the stainless steel bowl against the shiny sink.

"It's all good darling I'm just baking; you can go back to sleep."

Tucking his head onto his shoulder he shuffled further into his rug, continuing on with dreaming. He was showing his age on cold days now and that was why Jonah left him in the warmth of the house today. Throwing ingredients in order into the largest bowl without thinking, it was a breeze as she had made this recipe numerous times before. It was good when you have a favourite recipe that had been rehearsed so many times that it always turned out. Gemma had found that the trick was in the length of time the biscuits were left in the oven, and only just the right amount of colour should appear on the biscuit. Never overcooking them because as they cool they harden, so taking them out while still a little chewy worked best.

After the first two trays were cooling on the wire-racks the sweet aroma dispersed temptation around the entire house. It was time for a hot cuppa and a couple to test, yummy. Wilson's nose had been twitching while he slept with one eye open, taking in the mouth-watering sweet smells, chocolatey aroma wafted around the kitchen and he sat up when she pressed the blue light on the electric jug.

Breaking a biscuit in quarters ensured she carefully picked out the chocolate bits and consumed them herself before Wilson got the remaining plain crumbly bit. Completely aware that chocolate was poisonous to dogs. Still warm and inviting on this cold winters day, they tasted delicious, cognizant that there were still two more trays in the oven she kept watching while standing, sipping her hot coffee and peering out through the salt laden streaky kitchen window in hope of spotting Jonah arrive back soon.

Looking out over a dark soaked lone jetty bobbing around, the sea was no longer creeping but progressive waves were now lapping the bank, the forceful wind bending the willow tree branches enough for them to bop up and down lashing the salt water, splashes could be heard even in the kitchen as the branch hit the water surface with intensity, the weather had definitely worsened. Glancing up at the silver wall clock overhead it was already 11.30am, now Gemma was feeling anxious for Jonah to be home. She tightly clutched her warming mug of comforting coffee, wrapping her cold arthritic fingers around it, not only seeking the comfort of mobility but of emotional support, she was a bit worried.

"Let's sit in the bay window Wilson and wait for him eh?" one more biscuit for you. You're such a good dog." She bent down to pat him as he stood up to follow, before plonking himself to one side of the old armchair overlooking the backyard, she was grateful for his company.

Turning her attention onto the camellia hedge row, it was doing really well, attempting to offer up a little cheer with the cerise flowers reflecting a cherry brightness on this stormy dismal Saturday. Gentle rain started to slide down the windowpane blurring her view.

"Hurry home!" Gemma called out loudly, and Wilson lifted his head for a second to see if she was addressing him, before settling down again. Rushing to the kitchen she removed the final two trays of biscuits, resting them on wire racks before returning to the window to sit in hope of seeing *Jonah's Gem* returning to the jetty, which was now leaping up and down, bouncing off the surf.

Her eyes moved from the clock on the wall, straining to see through the windowpane as the trickles had turned into forceful pounding of heavy rain running down the glass. Gemma's sure no one else would choose to be out in this weather. It had worsened and her husband was still out there! The wind could be heard changing from a strong warning gust to crying out screaming gales, and now in the last five minutes its cries had turned to howls of pain, with trees blown sideways, one old pine tree let out a large crack as a branch of the old pine split and crashed to the ground, only a metre from the house. Gemma rushed to look around the house windows to get various viewpoints, her eyes straining, searching the violent waves for a glimpse of a boat. Nothing, she could not see *Jonah's Gem,* perhaps he found shelter and came ashore somewhere before reaching home. She sat down to pray he was safe, her eyes returning to the clock it was 12.05pm only 5 minutes since she last looked.

Grabbing the laptop lying on the coffee table she checked the weather forecast, hoping that the storm was expected to pass quickly. Desperation now filled her with fear; she watched as ripples across the screen showed the extent of storm coverage, beside warnings about the ferocity and staying away from the water. Gemma ran for her mobile and pushed emergency; she was put through to police Constable Greenslade who asked what the emergency was.

"Hello, this is Gemma Frederick I want to report my husband hasn't returned from his fishing, he went out at 10am in his boat, *Jonah's Gem* and planned to be back by now," struggling to keep a steady voice, it broke into a nervous crackle and her eyes filled with tears of panic.

"Where did he enter the sea, what's your address?" sounded the voice. "We might still be able to get the helicopter up depending on the wind speed, we'll alert the coast guard to check the shoreline and put out an alert. We haven't received any mayday radio contact from him, but we have turbulent seas now. I'll leave you with my contact cell phone number and keep you informed of any information coming to hand," came the concerned voice. "Stay near the phone and let us know straight away if he arrives home so we can call off the search." He says.

"Okay thanks," she said after giving their address and details. An upset shaky sound escaped, as the lump in her throat tightened not wanting to acknowledge she was filled with fear.

Hanging up she turned to Wilson, kneeling down beside him she reached her arms around his girth clinging on tightly while listening to the sound of howling turbulent wind blowing relentlessly outside. The trees continual groaning under the pressure as they bent endeavouring to avoid cracking, another succumbed to breaking point and crashed to the ground. The sky had darkened with horrifying black clouds in the distance.

All she could do was wait and listen to the roaring of the sea in the backyard, as it not only churned the once peaceful blue sea into a murky brown ocean full of debris, but it also churned her insides making her feel sick, heartbroken, as she thought of her husband out in that weather, *"Why did he have to go out today*? he loved his time on the boat but has unfortunately underestimated the power of nature." She spoke to herself and whispering her plea, "Please let Jonah be okay, you can turn the tide and calm the sea, please bring him home safety."

Checking the laptop, she then franticly tried to see through the windows, the forecast informed her of the storm prediction lasting the night, with high tides and dangerous beaches. She couldn't keep reading the screen as her eyes pooled with tears so shut it down to phone her daughter. Bridget answered straight away.

"Jonah's out in this storm, he hasn't come back after going out this morning," she hurriedly rattled off to her without pausing for breathe, panic threatening to overtake.

"Shall I drive up to see you mum?" she sounded concerned.

"No, it's too bad to be driving we'll have to wait until morning, to see if the search and rescue find him." The tears now ran down her face just like the outside of the windows.

"I'll be ready to drive as soon as the weather lets up okay. Stay positive, he'll be okay mum. He probably came ashore in some inlet somewhere to shelter in the boat, when he saw it getting too bad to get home. Has he phoned?" she asked.

"No, he doesn't answer his mobile I've been trying it all the time," Gemma cried out.

"He might have been too far out or could have lost the phone in the water with the rough seas," Bridget declared quite loudly.

"Or perhaps he has no signal eh." She tried to stay positive.

"Well, he knows the sea, he'll be fine." Attempting to reassure her mum. They were both afraid, fear sounded in their voices but were trying to stay positive in an appalling situation.

"Bye, I'll let you know if I hear something."

"Okay mum. Stay strong, I love you bye," says Bridget.

Restless, Gemma could not stay inside doing nothing. She once again attempted to peer through the rain streaked windows but it was pitch black outside now.

"Stay here Wilson, I'll be back soon, she pulled on heavy wet weather gear and headed for the back door of the house where the wind was not too bad, carefully making her way down to the jetty. Standing on solid ground and not venturing out onto the wooden structure in case she got swept into the sea, she shouted out.

"Jonah this way. Come home. I'm over here." With eyes searching, straining through the torrential rain and tears now streaming down her face, Gemma's determination was persistent but fraught with difficulty, as she screamed out as loud as she could with her heart pained, torn apart with fear as she prayed for her husband to return. Gemma's cries were getting blown away so she tried whistling a high pitch sound while the torrential rain was heavy on her head, cold water trickled down the inside of the waterproof gear, her clothes were soaked. She clung on, hugging tightly to a solid looking tree so as to keep her balance and not get blown over. Gemma's footing was dubious, what was once solid ground, had turned to slippery mud. Perhaps Jonah can not see the shore but she hoped he would hear her and know which way to go. Her anxiety continued to mount as she frantically wondered if his boat would stay afloat. The wind gusts were strong and blurred her eyes along with rain making her unable to see. Her clothes were wet through and her skin freezing cold, it was a struggle to stand and she knew it was hopeless.

      Tears of desperation and continuous rain mingled together as her stomach lurched, she was unable to endure the terror of worrying about him, ultimately she was forced to go back to the house feeling a hundred years old, as her breathing increased and she staggered to reach the side of the house to lean against, just before having a panic attack. Sheltering under the eaves with a bitterly cold wind blowing, she regained her breathe and could make out a dog's nose pressed against the windowpane. Wilson stood at the window his eyes pleading for her to return and she conceded defeat. The fierceness of the storm was frightening and she hastened to take care when opening the kitchen door so it was not wrenched out of her hands by strong gusts of wind.   Gloom and solicitude looking down at Wilson she accepted that she also had a duty of care to him.

      Forlornly stripping off the layers of weather proofing, the woollen jumper and trousers were dropped heavily sodden to the floor, shivering she grabbed a towel from the bathroom and rushed over to the warm fire. Thank goodness it continued to let out a welcoming warmth. Everywhere looked bleak, wet and she felt helpless, how must Jonah be feeling? After getting some circulation back into her extremities Gemma returned to deal with the sodden pile of wet clothes on the kitchen floor and with a frozen tear stained face, empty fear and loneliness engulfed her, she wrapped her arms around Wilson.

Chapter 13

Flashing across the television screen was a news special, Gemma sat down to watch it report a man missing out in the storm in his boat and a short written description of 'Jonah's Gem', her man! The world was being informed, so hopefully someone would find him, disillusioned and fearful this knowledge stirred her to stay positive. There were people looking and when morning dawned he would be home, he just had to survive the cold. Telling herself that as long as he was still on the boat and it had held up to the raging waves he would be okay. A crushing fear of hyperthermia bombarded Gemma as she knew that people died from it, mentally reassuring herself she saw him put on watertight clothes over his warm clothes and he took his thermos she had made for him. Fingers crossed that he stayed out of the deadly cold water. The sudden sound of swirling icy wind whistled around the house tormenting her, already sick from worry, it created anxiety, as though her insides were agonizingly, slowly being hauled out.

For something to do she boiled the electric jug yet again, making a cup of tea that she would probably not drink, all the time his beautiful songs ran around in her head, she was unable to get them out of her memories. Fear and mental fatigue sapped her energy, and she decided to stay warm on top of their bed, in close contact ready to leap to the phone if it rang from the bedside table. Sipping on the warm liquid helped to calm and clear her head a little, thawing and comforting as the phone finally rang.

"Hello," she shouted out expectantly.

"Hi Gemma, it's Stephan, I recognised the boat on the news. Is Jonah missing out in this storm?" he was hesitant to ask.

"Yes, it is Jonah out there. He failed to return from taking the boat out this morning." She rushed out a sad garbled explanation of the events.

"Don't worry, I'll contact the coast guard and offer any help I can."

"Thanks," she managed to say, before he hurriedly hung up and she stood, left disappointed that it wasn't better news.

Three o'clock in the afternoon and there was a knock on the door, she opened it to a group of searchers warmly clad with radios and mobiles in their hands, the men wore bright fluorescent clothes. All standing in groups each with an area mapped out to walk around the coast checking for any evidence of the boat or Jonah. Jeremy introduced himself, showing his identification from the search and rescue team, appearing to be expertly efficient provided her with a little reassurance and hope. Thanking him, she admitted that she felt relieved to know people were out looking, so hopefully her husband would be home soon. They looked blankly and advised that they would keep her informed.

Patricia, a kind 72 year old from next door also arrived to make her a hot drink, with her face pale and looking shocked she wrapped her arms around Gemma's trembling shoulders. She had been watching the news and came to see if Gemma was okay.

"No thanks, I can't drink any more, that's all I keep doing."

"You're okay, they'll find him." Patricia tried to reassure her neighbour because word had spread and even news reporters were driving around in marked vehicles. They stood in front of the jetty and filmed. Gemma found that intrusive but was prevented from objecting because she thought the more fishermen who knew about it would help. Everyone was doing their best to assist.

Patricia spoke, "The men have it under control you should go and get some rest; I'm just next door if you need me. Will you be okay?" she asked again, while wrestling with her wet raincoat.

"Yes, you go we just have to wait now." Gemma went over to sit by the window looking out to see boats being launched and crews of men walking over farmlands and around the water's edge, the tide had receded enough to walk around the rocks.

All eyes were searching as far as they could beyond the shore, silent impenetrable sadness surrounded Gemma as she succumbed to the comfort of cosy warm armchair tiredness, her eyes could no longer stay open, only waking up when her stomach grumbled from hunger pains, nothing except cups of tea all afternoon and incessant looking at the clock, it was teatime. Recalling how at lunch time she looked forward to her husband's return, eight hours later and she was still waiting. It was too lonely sitting alone at the dining table so she avoided doing so, she had eaten very little while deeply upset about Jonah being out there, somewhere! she just sat, sadly watching out of the window for his boat to return.

Her caring friend Helen, from the gardening club knocked on the door and insisted on staying with Gemma all night, saying she did not want her to be alone, Helen only lived five minutes down the road, and it was an incredibly kind offer which Gemma admitted that even though she had Wilson beside her, she appreciated someone to talk to, and welcomed her presence to help get a feel for what was happening, her emotions were all over the place. Helen went about getting them both toast as Gemma's body was under enough stress and enduring waves of a nightmarish headache as her heart and soul longed to see Jonah. The relentless torment and loneliness over how he might be suffering was worrying, and after nibbling a bit of toast for strength she was determined to try again. The rain had eased as she went out to look for her husband, she needed to stay positive and strong.

Leaving the house she shivered, not so much from cold but more from fear of the unknown and her hands trembled while gripping the side of the house wall, something took hold of her stomach as it clenched up and her lungs felt crushed, unable to breathe, tears ran in streams down a shocked face. Hearing screams she started to fight the arms that reached out to her.

"I pray he didn't fall overboard in the storm," she cried to Helen.

That useless thought crept into her mind sometimes, and as the day drew to an end she clung to hope, refusing to allow her energy to wane from the crushing weight of fear, but also remembering Jonah had said he needed a more powerful motor. Silently, unspoken they all knew, every day he was missing at sea his chances of survival withered. Helen attempted to get Gemma back inside the house.

"No, I don't need you, let me go, it's all okay he's not lost at sea he'll be home soon," screaming and out of control Gemma struggled to push her friend away, like a woman possessed. Suddenly everything was spinning around her and then it all stopped!

Waking up on top of the bed with the sun rising she had no memory of how she got there, and then she saw the harbour patrol boat through the bedroom window and her daughter Bridget standing beside the bed. Nausea took hold and then a rush of vomit threatened, Gemma rushed to the toilet, too emotionally exhausted to weep any more, fear had stolen her energy and her head was pounding, she just wanted Jonah to be home.

Heading for the kitchen to find some pain relief for her headache, also aware that nothing would relieve the ache of her heart and panic in her soul. Bridget followed her back to sit on the edge of the bed, but Gemma was oblivious to the words coming from her daughter. Looking out of the window it was a nice warm, sunny day today while her world was dissolving like a block of ice in the hot sun. Then, she was aware of Wilson who came running in from outside, she was so thrilled to see him. He rested his chin over her legs and then rose up to give her a slurpee kiss across her face, she wrapped her arms around him with a grateful smile.

"Thank goodness for Wilson, hello little guy." Smiling down at an affectionate furry friend.

Bridget spoke, "You haven't been eating properly and you collapsed outside late last night, luckily your friend Helen phoned me and helped get you into bed."

"I'm okay, have they found the boat yet?" she asked.

"No nothing." Sadness prevalent in her voice.

Gemma sat lugubriously contemplating life and how no matter what happens to us all, the tide will continue to ebb and flow, the feathered birds will fly above and the sunrays will again shine down, these things gave hope for another day, hope for a better future and another chance at love, surrounded by ordinary things and familiar people, but she already had it all and now she wanted to escape this life of uncertainty and unpredictable heartbreak. She wanted to run back to the cottage, then she remembered what Jonah always said; *'The pain you feel is proof that you have felt love and have lived life, you don't want to miss out on that!'*

He would come back to her, she believed it, she felt it.

Meanwhile somewhere out at sea *Jonah's gem* was being tossed like a toy boat in a glass bottle, his struggle so tough that he had become disorientated and had no idea where he was anymore. The compass was unstable as he attempted to read it; some equipment had been washed away as the waves tilted the boat. He studied the way the sea dragged him out into the immense darker ocean beyond, he reasoned he must be headed north after the morning light rose, but he was certain he was lost now as he should be going south to get home. Struggling to turn the stern of the boat around, the motor was not powerful enough against the waves; terrified, he could see a huge wave on the horizon accelerating towards *Jonah's Gem* and was about to strike the boat side on.

Quickly threading the rope he uses for mooring, through the closest wooden slot in the flooring he tied himself to the other end of the stout rope, he prayed to the powers that be, to help him to survive. Crashing and swishing of strong waves forced one side of the boat to rear up out of the water too far to return back down again, water flooded into the boat, the weight of which caused it to tip over, before the next wave hit in quick succession.

Then sudden calmness between the waves allowed Jonah to pause, finding himself thrown into pitch black, unable to see he felt around and following the rope he used to tie himself to the floor. The floor now above him, his head was out of the sea water but his body was submerged in freezing cold water. Figuring that he had to be in an air pocket under the capsized boat, he held tight while considering what to do. There was no way he could right the boat, it would be impossible to turn it over by himself, he knew that was not an option. He was safe there for now, except for the cold and the unknown, how long would the air last, or even if another wave would sweep him and the boat further out to goodness knows where.

Fear now had a hold over him in the deep abyss of immense ocean, one man on his own in complete darkness with the very real threat of hyperthermia setting in. Floating in freezing conditions his mind became a foggy haze, loneliness and panic stricken, only alert enough to comprehend his situation was dire, he wondered how he could have been so foolish and thought of his wife, Gemma.

A strong will and determination to get back to her took hold as he struggled to think. 'I'll climb on top of the upturned boat, someone will see the boat from the air, I just have to hold on until the weather improves.' Undoing the rope from the floorboard hanging down above him, he shrugged off heavy clothes and took a large gulp of air, he timed his return to the surface between the waves, swimming as strongly as possible through the salt water, while it stung at his eyes he didn't care as he headed toward the light he could see flickering up top. Surging overhead he swam out quickly rising between waves, he grabbed at the still outboard motor quickly wrapping the loose end of rope around it and he watched fearfully as another wave came billowing towards him, about to hit.

A strong forceful yank on the rope burned at his waist as the boat was pushed along with each wave, he was pulled along with it.

Enduring painful rope burns he yelled in pain while not giving up, he must stay tied to *Jonah's Gem*, it was a lifeline to being seen from above in the cold darkness. After each wave he climbed back on top of the overturned boat, out of the cold water while he was continually swept off. What seemed like hour after hour he continued to climb back onto the boat again and again, aware of the danger of hyperthermia he must get through the cold dark deepening blackness, certain that the dawning of morning would bring with it more opportunity. The strength of the sea began to wain as did Jonah's strength and the will to go on, all he had left was the durability of the rope and his unyielding memories and love for Gemma waiting for his return.

When morning finally shone down the ocean was calm, and at first he welcomed the warmth of the drying sun penetrating through his sodden clothes, as he once again lay on the overturned boat knowing he had beaten hyperthermia. As the challenge continued hour after hour, the day dragged on and he did not hear any sound, no plane or boat as any hope of survival started to diminish, his energy exhausted, no food and no water was affecting his cognitive abilities, and he realized that he could no longer think straight, he started to speak out loud just to keep words in his head, trying to retain the ability to string an intelligent sentence together.

Dehydration was his next hurdle, it was disparaging to have come this far in his battle surrounded by ocean, when drinking water, a life giving necessity was nowhere to be found. He longed for the coffee flask locked in the boat food storage cupboard and he forced himself to think, plan how to get it. Sitting up, one leg draped either side of the hull, he sat comfortably now with calm rippling waters. After surviving being trapped under the boat he was terrified of going back down into the dark water in case he never returned, grateful for the warmth of the sun, but equally aware that it was also deadly. He struggled to think clearly and carefully went over a plan in his head to clarify if it would work. Looking at the sea, which was now calm, he then turned to the motor, which was old, he checked to see if he could unscrew the blade, it was too tight without the proper tools and having little strength, then he saw the rope that secured him to the motor. Carefully undoing the end from the motor he wrapped it around the large round screw, and with the other end still tied around his waist he used the whole of his body to pull. It slowly started to spin and the old shaft became wobbly, he kept working on it until the screw broke off, lifting the shaft out of its position and meticulously working back and forth until the blade came off.

    Breathing a sigh of relief, exhausted Jonah carefully worked out where the cupboard would be under the boat now that it was upside down. Decidedly confident of its position, he started to bash hard at that spot, with the blade held carefully in his shaky hands, steady determination and hope in his heart he persisted, driven by the belief he might have a chance of getting home to Gemma, his thirst so grave now that he had a choking cough, until a glimpse of expectation ran through his veins. A small crack appeared in the wooden boat, bending over very carefully he pressed an eye to the hole in an effort to see through, yes! the metal flask shimmered with the small amount of reflected light sneaking in. Renewed, he pounded the floor more profoundly now with new vigour, persistence and adrenalin rush.

    Reaching in, he slowly pulled the coffee flask gently through the hole he had made and sat gratified, with shaky hands he carefully unscrewed the top, it was still a little bit warm, wet and sweet, the coffee, milk and caffeine a delight for a burst of energy.

    Lifting the flask into the air, "Thank you love," he yelled.

    Finally after a drink, he knew his chance of survival would increase as he took careful sips, only when he had to. Elated he spotted land a long way off, but he had no idea where he was.

    Bridget settled her small bag in the spare room, "I'm staying here with you tonight mum," she called from the bedroom.

"Okay, you'll find everything you need in the linen cupboard to make up the bed." Gemma welcomed her presence.

Then returning to the kitchen Bridget opened the freezer, she removed two microwave steak pies and started to prepare kumara, sliced thinly and dropped them into a pot of water, tipping a small amount of frozen mixed vegetables into the same pot.

"You need to eat a meal and look after yourself mum, it's no good getting sick. Then you won't be any use to Jonah when he's found, will you?" she said kindly but sternly.

"I'm okay." Gemma was starting to weep, an awful heart wrenching sigh escaped from the depths of anguish, as the desperation of not knowing where Jonah was, and what horror he was suffering now overwhelmed her.

"He'll be found mum; the storm has gone and the weather is improving." She put her arm around her mum and they hugged before making a strong cup of tea, taking it over to sit by the window overlooking the jetty. The day was awfully long without any news.

A second night followed, they both succumbed to fatigue from waiting, hoping for some positive news. Gemma faced another night of torment, alone in bed wondering what Jonah was going through, was he still alive? Just as she drifted in and out of some semblance of sleep, light forced its way through the curtains like an unwanted intruder at the crack of dawn and another morning arrived uninvited.

Still fatigued from enduring the bleakest lingering night of her life, with no phone call from the police or anyone to say he had been found. It was early when at first light she crept out of bed ready, weak and shaky after being unable to stomach any pie and vegetables that Bridget had thoughtfully prepared the night before. With little sleep and desperately wanting Jonah to be found today, to have him safely home was all she wanted. Gemma's body and spirit weighed heavily, tiredness and loneliness seeping through her veins and a heavy emotional fatigue sapping her energy as they waited to hear any news.

Jonah and Gemma always saw the wood behind the trees, and appreciated taking time to stop and observe nature, admiring the beauty of flowers in the garden, new growth in their orchard and copious fresh fruit to feed them. Reminiscing helped Gemma to stay positive and believe that nature would not take him from her. Jonah could not die, the best thing that ever happened to her was falling in love with him. She remembered when she never wanted to marry again, but Jonah won her heart and now look, she was so afraid the love of her life had been taken by the sea.

He was out in his boat doing what he enjoyed doing, she told herself, at least he was not in a car crash. Gemma was adamant that he would be found, he would be and she refused to let doubt or fear control her. Jonah would be driven to get back to her. Yet another morning arrived, following a dismal but cloudless night came another day of optimism and searching, while they sat keeping vigil the sea remained calm, the winds had gone and even the early sunshine was now relentlessly pounding heat onto the searchers. Late afternoon there was a knock at the door.

Bridget rushed to open it with Gemma right behind her, there was a constable standing waiting, his tired sweaty face depicting the doleful duty and stress he was also under. Fear swept through Gemma unable to face what he had to say, her face pale listening as he solemnly spoke.

"We've found a man washed up on the shore, he's in a bad way and being taken to the hospital. Can you come and see if it's your husband please." He spoke with a kind softness.

Relief flooded over Gemma while her head spun round and her heartbeat faster in a panic, all at the same time. She trusted it would be her husband; she had prayed so hard for him to be found alive, but how is he in a bad way, what does that mean?

"Yes, I'll drive mum," Bridget said hurriedly, while Gemma sprinted around the kitchen wondering what to do. They grabbed handbags and mobiles, hastily putting Wilson outside and locking up the house, Bridget drove the small Honda to the hospital while they were in a flutter wanting to get there as quickly as possible. He's been found!

Bridget showed the way through the long corridors as Gemma fought for control over her pounding heart and nervousness. The staff would only allow two people to go into the room, lying on the hospital bed only covered with a light sheet they were confronted with an alarming sight. A hardly recognisable person, his face badly sunburnt with sunken cheeks defining the bones, shrivelled hands from being too long in the saltwater had the skin flaking and peeling off, and the putrid smell of rotting flesh was also evident around the sterile room mingling with the hospital smells, his extremely thin neck showing above the white hospital sheet was also red raw, it was Jonah but he was very dehydration and emaciated.

"Oh my darling what has happened to you?" Gemma cried out, afraid to touch this fragile man with his long fingers shrivelled and painfully red sore with just a thin covering of damaged wrinkled skin. In just a few days, how could he get this bad she cried as she carefully laid her face gently on the top of his lank hair, afraid to touch any part of him in case it hurt him, his skin barely attached. Her eyes glossed over and she started to tear up, overflowing to silently trickle down her face. Wiping them away with one hand and trying to be brave for him as he lay with his eyes closed.

"You'll be okay, you're safe now," she whispered into his ear.

His eyes opened but he didn't speak, their eyes delving deeply into each other, his love transcending right through her body. Gently patting his hair down she was distraught to see him this way, and Gemma could only imagine his pain. She wanted to crawl in beside him and keep hugging him until he was better, never to let him go.

"Do you recognise him as being Jonah?" Constable Greenslade entered the room.

"Yes, he is my husband, what happened to him?" she longed to know, deeply concerned about how long it will take for him to recover.

"We found his boat *'Jonah's Gem'* capsized, he either swam ashore or was washed up, it's a miracle as he's used up all of his reserves to battle the tide, getting out of the salt water. He's exhausted and we don't know how he managed to get back to land. Fortunately, he was wearing a life jacket and a farmer found him washed up, wedged between gaps in the rocks at the bottom of a paddock. He said he never normally goes that close to the sea, except he has on inquisitive puppy who was sniffing around the craggy rocks and started barking at this bundle of damaged body, he still had that life jacket on." Pointing to a battered, dirty bright orange lump lying on the chair.

"So the farmer climbed down the bank when he caught a glimpse of the florescent orange. It probably saved your husband's life," he commented.

Gemma carefully lifted Jonah's frail damaged hand to lie on top of hers, somehow he appeared much older than when he set off three days ago, words failed her because there were no words, just relief as she whispered his name and gently squeezed the underside of his hand. Bridget scrapped a chair across the polished floor in that little hushed room for Gemma to sit beside her husband. In silence, she was so grateful to have him back and respectful of his dreadful ordeal and terrible injuries. Bridget sat on the opposite side of the bed after putting a cup of tea in Gemma's spare hand as they looked at each other, silently imagining the terrible pain he must be enduring with his burns and yet Gemma felt less anxious, filled with relief now that he was back, she was resolute to help him recover. He was alive.

It was unbearable to watch and to hold back the tears so she stood up, gently setting her cup down on the chair Gemma excused herself and left the room to stand outside in the corridor, she needed time to pull herself together, to find the courage for her man.

Holding onto the door frame with shaking body she was like a popped balloon, deflated and shocked she clung to the timber frame for strength. When she returned to the room the doctor was waiting, he began to explain how the skin would repair itself, the intravenous drip would hydrate Jonah, he had not eaten anything for three days so was being fed slowly on special food at first.

He went on to explain, "There are cuts and bruises to heal but he should be okay. The main concern are the kidneys not having had any water for so long, we're testing him to see if there is any kidney damage."

Jonah's determination had brought him home and he would get well again, he'll be okay. He murmured something and the nurse helped to prop him up, Jonah lightly squeezed her hand and she began to cry, Bridget quietly got up and left the room so they could be alone together. Grief stricken after the ordeal he had been through, they were both relieved as she kissed his lips very carefully, he managed a pained smile and she could already see the little twinkle coming back into his eyes. The nurse advised them to let him rest now and see him tomorrow when he would feel better after the fluids and pain medication for his sunburn.

Kissing him goodbye, "Thank goodness you got back, you're going to be okay," Gemma whispered to him.

Gently patting his chest, the only bit that was covered by his lifejacket, with skin peeling off everywhere else, the harsh drying of the salt water and scorching sun had done a lot of damage. He lay wrapped in compression bandages but his eyes were following her.

In that surreal moment they were at peace and he quietly murmured his love for her; he lifted his hand slowly to stroke her hair before his strength was gone and he fell off to sleep.

Gemma was now aware of Bridget's presence touching her back, "Come on mum," she says. "Let's take you home, he's alright, let him get some sleep it's the best thing for his recovery."

Looking up at her concerned face, Gemma was suddenly mindful and grateful that her daughter had been there for her, Bridget wrapped her arm around Gemma's shoulders and guided her to the door. Leaving him was tough but she had too, he needed to rest. Bridget drove them safely back home, only to discover many well wishes had left cards and flowers at the front door.

"I'll phone around and thank them but I'm sure Jonah doesn't want visitors at the moment while he looks so bad." Bridget stated. She would go and thank the neighbours for dropping in food and helping in the search.

Hearing her words but not answering, Gemma rushed to the bathroom for an escape, it had been traumatic and clinging on tightly to the hand basin her chest heaved, as the tears flowed. Relief, and also upset at his appearance and the pain he had endured chilled her to the bone, as every part of her began to quiver. Flash backs of his injuries haunted her mind as she recalled how the craggy dehydrated skin on bone was shrivelled like a dried apricot, all the liquid gone and sore flesh was stretched like plastic wrap over a plate of leftovers. It was distressing to think he went through being lost and not knowing if they would ever be together again, her poor husband had been through so much trauma and love and determination had won out, she was proud of him for his effort and his devotion to her.

She could never imagine his torment, trying to imagine the pain radiating through his body, comparing the time she got a bit sun burnt on her back, which was painfully hot the first night then as it healed it went itchy before peeling off; or perhaps he hurts like her finger did when it accidently touched the element on the stove, oh Jonah, she couldn't imagine! With the extent and depth of damage done she trusted the hospital would give masses of pain relief so he wouldn't endure anymore now that he was safe.

Chapter 14

Climbing into bed that night her thoughts were constantly with Jonah, her mind actively running over what if? It all became too much and she felt panicked; it was unbearable so she got out of bed and went to see Bridget in the next room.

Looking up from her pillow, "What's wrong mum?" she asked.

"I can't sleep because we should have found him earlier!"

"We all tried, we did our best, don't think about him hurt and suffering, think about when he will be better," she says. "He will get well and be home soon."

"Yes, he will." Comforted she went back to bed.

Visits to the hospital watching his struggle were hard, but it was even harder being at home without him. Gemma's neighbour Patricia had become a good friend popping in with home baking and flowers from her garden while checking in on her, she constantly reinforced that it wouldn't be long before Jonah was home again.

Many long days of sitting with Jonah had seen the winter vanish and slowly he had become able to focus pain free, sometimes listening to an audio book while Gemma snatched a few minutes to leave the suffocating smells of the hospital, to walk around in the cool spring air outside. Jonah was still unable to leave the hospital he was too weak, and his new fragile baby skin was unable to have any sunlight on it. When they were not together Gemma felt like a car running on empty, having no reserves or enthusiasm to even work in the garden, she had taken to writing while home alone, hopeful that he would be amused when he edited her work later on, she missed him dreadfully, he was her other half and she worried about him.

When he was found the news spread quickly in the newspapers, radio and television, being found alive was the amazing phenomenon that everyone had wished for and it was nice to have happy news, although she was unsure of how she felt about their quiet lives suddenly becoming so public. She decided that as long as he was protected from visitors while in the hospital recovering, it was of no importance, and eventually another newsworthy event would come along and take the attention away from Jonah. People were kind and well wishes encouraged him psychologically to cheer up and get well. Suddenly aware now that perhaps she was like everyone else, as she always watched the news and longed for the lost one to be found, in some small way it was like the worlds arms were reaching out to hug them all, as part of a bigger caring community.

Slowly life improved for Jonah, who was accepting of his appearance and welcomed his friend Mike and fishing buddy Stephan to visit him in hospital. That always cheered him up, and watching him laughing with his mates was heart-warming, offering up a semblance of normality once again. Stephan has retrieved *Jonahs Gem* and stored it in the boathouse for later, they were both grateful but it was not something they wanted to talk about, or to even face at the moment.

Waking up on Saturday morning Gemma stumbled a little before sitting on the edge of the bed, perhaps she needed to eat more as she had lost her appetite for a while now. She knew that Jonah would have his friends to visit him today so decided to take it easy. Gemma had so much to be grateful for and decided to go and visit the old church they got married in. It was not a hot day, so Wilson would be fine left in the car with his water bowl and the window down a little. She proceeded to walk the length of the picket fence observing how all the hydrangeas had buds of shiny green leaves starting to burst into life. Standing in the entrance looking out over the street filled with modern homes, here stood a little old church displaying a simple elegance of times gone by, when small was appreciated and people did not want big or grand. The tranquil spiritual grace was sensed around this beautiful little church where they were married. She paused to breath and appreciate the ambience before gently pushing open the double red doors which were slightly ajar, each footstep, the only sound heard on the solid polished floor as she slipped reverently into the back row of solid kauri pews, looking up to note the faded red velvet drapes that had withstood the test of time, enduring scorching rays coming down through glazed leadlight arches, high up on the wood panel walls. Gemma tilted her head to give thanks for Jonah and for the miracle of his return. She lost track of time in that solid building that had stood strong and from another era when she decided it must be time to leave. Back in her car she was welcomed with a wet nose coming through from the back seat nudging her back into the present.

    She was overcome by a deep desire and compulsion to visit her cottage by the sea, so she began to drive another 35km to check on it. Gemma had not been to stay over the winter while Jonah was unwell. Wilson enthusiastically leapt out of the car as soon as the car door swung open for him, he had never forgotten this home he and Gemma lived in for all of his puppy life. She searched on the key ring, fumbling with the old worn key, it was comfortable in her hand and she couldn't wait to hurry around the back of the cottage to see how her garden was coping. She sat on the park bench taking time to breath in the sweet smells of the flowers that had been self-seeding everywhere and one after the other had kept on thriving, the beautiful flowers always inspired her, even though some were short lived, they made the most of everyday flourishing, before they died.

    "Oh why can't things live longer, why can't I feel happiness for a bit longer, I need Jonah to get well, I miss him terribly." She rested and muttered her thoughts out loud. The peace and serenity of this place gave her the security and permission to cry, her other half was absent, still in hospital. After the expedient release of tears and contemplation she eventually stood up, slowly so as not to become dizzy. There was no way they could leave without taking Wilson for a run in the familiar safety of the park, with its memories of the years living in solitude and safety where she couldn't be hurt; dwarfed by the giant Puhutakawa tree she watched him run in the park while

Jonah's words echoed in her mind, he always said that any pain felt, was not something to be sad about, it was an acknowledgement she lived life. What wonderful memories she had stored away in the back of my mind because of the presence and mindfulness of love, life and their beautiful relationship.

September did slowly follow on from August and as she visited the hospital this morning the doctor finished his rounds and gave Jonah the good news, he was finally well enough to go home the following week. He was ordered to keep the compression bandages on, and drink plenty to hydrate not only the skin but also to keep his kidneys functioning, he had been very lucky that both were unaffected by the extreme dehydration he had suffered. He was healed enough to return home, Gemma was over the moon, and apart from emotionally and a few physical scars Jonah was well and would return home. The sun shone on his return home it was a promising spring day, back together again. With his arms wrapped around Gemma and the warmth of their bodies together at night, relief encased them both and they could rest contentedly.

Wonderful days spent going for a drive and visiting Bridget, occasionally she would meet up at the cottage on a weekend to give her little spaniel a run in the park. Life became slower, tranquilly more important somehow, making each day full of time together. Neither of them has wanted to look at 'Jonah's Gem' that nearly took Jonah's life; it stayed stored in the boathouse, apparently undamaged apart from the hole in the floor that Jonah made to reach the flask. They never wanted to talk about the boat and the almost fatal mistake that he made going out in rough weather, it was still too painful to even think about what happened.

When he came home Jonah repeatedly said how sorry he was for the boating incident, and Gemma asked him not to speak of it, he was a wonderful kind man and a fantastic husband.

Life was good, so she was surprised when getting up out of bed one morning her head was whirling and quiet dizzy, she slumped back down onto the beautiful cream and gold duvet, she decided to stand up slower the second time. Luckily, Jonah was in the kitchen making a cup of tea for them both. Gemma didn't want to worry him as it was probably nothing, she had been through so much stress, fearing that Jonah may have drowned at sea and going through his recovery with him, perhaps it had all been a bit much, they weren't young anymore and she would take time to get over it. Gemma's appetite had returned this morning so everything should be back to normal, cooking their favourite recipes again.

There was a knock on the door, she went to open it and welcomed Jonah's friend Stephan.

"Hi, how's the patient?" he asks with a lofty little laugh.

"Oh he's doing well, come on in Jonah's in the kitchen."

A screeching noise from the feet of the bar stool filled the entire room as Stephan pulled it out from under the breakfast bar. He sat and observed Jonah rummaging in the kitchen.

"Oh hi Stephan, do you want a coffee?" he looked up from dropping hot charred toast onto a plate.

"Hi, no thanks Jonah, how are you doing? I'm taking the boat out this afternoon would you like to keep me company?" he offers.

"Oh, I haven't been back on the water since the storm," Jonah replied quite seriously, glancing over at Gemma.

"It's a lovely day Jonah and you're not on your own. Grab your fishing rod and just go for a short time," Stephan suggested.

"Thanks for the offer Stephan, another time but not today." He shook his head.

"Okay, I always welcome a fishing buddy on board, so just let me know anytime you want to come."

"I will thank you." Smiled Jonah

After a chat about small motors and things men chat about he got up to leave, calling out as he reached the front door. "Bye Gemma."

"Bye, see you again soon," she called back to him.

Jonah had been languishing around the place for a month now, standing at the jetty and longingly looking out to sea, he had not been into the shed to see *Jonah's Gem*, which was in fine condition. His buddies had been and replaced the motor blade and repaired the broken floor he bashed a hole in. But he was finding that not going out on the water was difficult, and Gemma had noticed his uncertainty, she could understand how hard it would be for her not to pursue gardening. Everyone needed to do the things they loved.

Gemma found it tortuous to watch the yearning in Jonah's eyes when he wanting to go out, she wondered if it was duty to her or fear restricting him. Sometimes it was upsetting to watch the anguished look in his eyes and she didn't know how to approach the subject and hoped that he would get over it.

Physically Jonah had healed but the doctor has made an appointment for him to see a councillor, to talk about being lost at sea and the trauma he suffered. Last week at his check-up it was revealed that he has been diagnosed with Post Traumatic Stress Disorder as Gemma sat waiting in the doctor's reception room Jonah talked about the recurring nightmare he had.

At home he had spoken to Gemma about being trapped under the boat and the red hot burning of his skin, he explained how he thought he was going to die and felt guilty for going out and leaving her when he shouldn't have. His nightmare of swimming through the tide to take him ashore after watching, planning and impatiently waiting for the high tied mark when he could see a lot of beach and then a little beach. He worked out when the tide was right to help push him ashore, he told Gemma of his fear. How reluctantly he untied himself from the safety of the boat and let go of it, uncertain if he would make it back.

Once the struggle of swimming ashore was successful then he kept being thrashed against the rocks, he had no more strength to fight and thought that was the end, he was near death. He said he forced his mind back to picture their wedding day and then Gemma standing, waiting at the jetty for his return. Fixing that picture in his mind keeping him alive, only now it persisted and wouldn't go away, it had become a recurring nightmare.

They drove home hardly saying anything after the doctors visit.

"My darling, I don't blame you for what happened, it was a mistake and its history now, we need to forget about it, we're back together again." She walked into the kitchen.

Jonah followed her and pulled Gemma close to him, hugging her tightly like he never wanted to let her go.

"I don't know if I will ever go back into the boat, I might sell it," he says.

"Whatever you want to do is okay with me, I know it'll never happen again, you'll be more cautious in the future if you do decide to go fishing again one day. I'm happy for you to do so."

There was no reply, Jonah just looked thoughtful and undecided.

"Well, if you're not going out with Stephan, let's go off to the garden centre for lunch and have a look around, do you want to do that?" she asked.

"Yes that's a good idea, after we wonder around our orchard to see what's happening out there eh." He smiled.

Wilson was already madly tearing around in the orchard as they walked quietly hand in hand mindful that they have both survived the winter and now spring showers were upon them with new delights to enjoy together. They saunter over lush soft grass underfoot breathing in the satisfying smell of sweet clean smelling citrus flowers mingled with crisp sea breeze, all overseen by a welcoming yellow ball of warmth just rising in the sky. Gemma was no longer feeling lost, sad or lonely they were back together admiring how well everything was growing. The subtle spring warmth was pushing tiny shapes of joyously pleasing and delicious plums, peaches and succulent fruits from dormant wood to provide plentiful fresh fruit for summer. The orchard provided them not only with food but they reap pleasure as it constantly changes with the seasons. They had placed a small round aluminium table along with matching grey chairs between the shade giving trees, positioned already for the promise of hot summer sun so they would always enjoy a rest in between strolling hand in hand. They deviate as they come upon the daffodil lined driveway, this year being better than ever with multiple whites, cream, pinks and yellows in a variety of petals and cups making an absolutely bountiful display of beautiful colour. Strolling along content in the joint decision to plant them in the lawn, which made it so easy to mow over at the end of their short flowering life enjoying the massive display while it lasted.

Three months flew past faster than they would have liked in their little slice of paradise. Not saying anything to Jonah, Gemma was finding that first thing in the morning the dizziness was still with her. On the morning walk they have started an unintentional habit of carrying a large cane basket around to pick a mixture of berry fruit, they found it useful as they often gather a variety of nice fruits to have with cheese and crackers for lunch later on, particularly nice on a hot day.

"Look at Wilson, with his nose pushing around in the strawberry plants what's he doing? did he see a skink to chase do you think?"

Wilson gave a little tug with his head and appeared with the nicest reddest strawberry in his mouth and slowly meticulously devoured it with juice running down his chin and a look of great satisfaction on his face.

"He likes strawberries!" Exclaimed Jonah.

"Oh no when did he discover that?" she laughed.

"I don't know, but it doesn't matter, we can close the gate and we can have a few laughs watching him, we have plenty don't worry." They both laughed in amazement at the way he enjoyed the sweet juice in his mouth, the expression was priceless.

"Oh my goodness, a dog that loves fruit, what next," Gemma exclaimed light heartedly.

Jonah has now finished with his doctor's appointments and seemed to have dealt with the post-traumatic stress as he slept better. He had settled back into a routine enjoying home life, a once a week outing to dance and his good friends visiting, the boat remained sheltering in the old boat house and provided a roof for Shed Cat who always stayed well clear of Wilson.

"Jonah, now your health is sorted I think I should go to the doctor to see why I'm getting dizzy; I had put it down to the stress of you being ill but it doesn't seem to be going away." Gemma began to explain during the walk back to the house.

"Okay, and I notice you have lost weight as well. Try to get an appointment to go next week, it pays to check things out." He smiled and gave her arm a compassionate squeeze.

Life was grand, spending time walking every day. Relishing the quiet life and never speaking about the boat. That was Jonah's decision to deal with in his own way and in his own time.

She enjoyed the many outings they went on together and Jonah liked to take her out to the garden centres for lunch. Every couple of months they put Wilson in the kennels for a holiday while they went away for a couple of days to explore the many beautiful gardens and scenery around New Zealand, providing them with exciting new ideas to try out in their own garden.

"Jonah can you help me trim back the Albezia shade tree on the back lawn today? It's not dormant but it needs to be shortened a bit, it's easy to see where it needs the length of branches shortened to encourage more side shoots. It'll be a lovely umbrella tree for shade next summer," Gemma beseeched over breakfast.

"Yes, is that the weeping tree that has the flurry of pretty pink flowers that drop little threads of bloom? he asked.

"Yes, it's very pretty isn't it?" she smiled back.

"I'll get the ladder; we don't want to take much off it though do we?"

"Not much, just a little off each arching branch to thicken it up. I have plans for another seating place under it."

He looked across with surprise and they both laughed. Jonah knew she loved to sit around the garden, moving around to sit in the shade or in winter to find the morning sun. Always spending more time out than in, she loved the outdoors.

The two of them had a shared interest and appreciation of time in the garden together, the memories and joy they both got from watching the birdlife and how everything evolved providing an unlimited refuge.

Gemma had a quick visit to the doctor, when explaining the fatigue and dizziness and asking his opinion he looked concerned as he thumbed his way through her family history.

"Your mother had Acute Myeloid Leukaemia which is most common in those older than 65 years. So I'm just going to get a blood test done to rule that out, okay," he said as he looked up from the file on his desk.

Stunned for a second, she paused before answering; "I wasn't expecting such an awful thought," she said. "Okay then, I'm sure I'm just a bit run down."

"A simple blood test will tell us, I want to check out the dizziness, fatigue and your pale skin and painful joints, you also appear to bruise easily." Looking up he handed her the referral form to take to the laboratory.

"You could get it done right now before you go home," he suggested. Pointing to the lab next door. Collecting her dusky pink handbag from the floor and thanking him she proceeded to the reception desk, before going into the laboratory. Her hands were shaking; she hadn't linked the dizziness with her mums leukaemia.

Chapter 15

Arriving home, Jonah was reclining in a chair looking out to sea and Gemma headed straight for the safety of the bedroom to put away her handbag and swap her good shoes for a comfy pair, what could she say? Concerned that she didn't greet him when arriving through the front door he appeared in the doorway of their bedroom.

"How did you get on at the doctors?"

"He sent me for a blood test to check everything, and I have to ring up for the results next week." Gemma explained with a smile, not wanting to speculate on something that might not happen.

"That's good, I'll make us a cuppa," he called back and as he turned towards the kitchen, Gemma knew how lucky she was to have such a protective husband.

Every so often the two of them plus Wilson, enjoyed weekends at the cottage, although not her home anymore. All of her favourite plants were now planted at Number 8, they have created a new rose garden with a terracotta pathway, Gemma loved to wander around taking in all of the different scents; lemon, sweet jasmine, floral roses and scented geranium standing under the fragrant exotic scented frangipani tree with small drifting yellow eyed white stars falling into her hair now with the change of season.

Comforting nights were spent with Gemma leaning back against Jonah in bed, content as she drifted off to sleep, they appreciated being together more than ever, nothing taken for granted, together they relished the warm safety in each other's arms.

Everyday was good, as she tried to put the doctor's suspicions out of her mind, she believed that everything would be fine, they were destined to stay together and she couldn't bear anymore trauma happening to either of them.

Friday evening approached and they decided on a quick tea of mince pies and chips heated in the oven so they could shower and get ready for the usual fun night out at the dance club. The couples have changed over the years with some moving away, others had become too old and sick to dance, however, they continued to meet new people all the time.

Timothy and Kirsty spotted them, remembered from last week, smiling they made their way over to share a table, they were a lovely young couple, in their late 40s their kids had flown the nest and now was their time to enjoy together in between work and sometimes babysitting three grandchildren. Their dancing was a bit clumsy but they were getting the hang of it. Every move took time and practice; they all relaxed with a drink to watch the others and attempted to learn something new each week while having a laugh.

Jonah loved to explore the internet and often came up with a move he wanted to learn. Their spare room with its polished floor was perfect, so Gemma sometimes set up the device, and tuned into some good music in a quest to slowly practice over and over until satisfied that they had mastered the new move. It was so much fun, and kept them young, fit and laughing a lot as each year seemed to accelerate by too quickly. Out on the dance floor with a dozen other couples all whirling around on a Friday night, Jonah's arm tightened around her waist as she wobbled a bit, he prevented her from falling.

"Are you okay?" looking down at her. "What happened?" he asked.

"Nothing, just a bit dizzy," Gemma reassured him that she was fine as they went to sit down.

Jonah was too apprehensive to try spinning her around anymore during the dances, so they decided to make it an early night and after saying goodbye to the others they headed home for a cup of tea and regrettably settle for a movie instead.

Saturday morning Jonah jumped out of bed and insisted on bringing her a cuppa in bed which was a great excuse for snuggling down for extra cuddles and a slow start to the day. The weather was brilliant outside and after taking Wilson for a run around the bountiful orchard they just pottered about in the garden and mowed the lawns. A roast chicken dinner went down nicely and finished with French vanilla ice-cream, stacking the dishwasher then both blobbing out in front of the television. Gemma had not been light-headed all day, however Jonah insisted that she phone and check on the blood test results on Monday, in the hope of them being back.

Gemma's mobile rang, "Hello," she called down the line.

"Hi mum its Carl."

"Oh, this is a surprise I haven't heard from you for ages," she squealed, thrilled.

"I'm sorry mum, but with work and living in Christchurch, I know I should make more time to phone but just never get around to it. Anyway Sue and I are coming up to visit you and Jonah next week we have something important to tell you."

"Oh, is everything alright with you both?" Panic slithered down her spine.

"Yes, don't worry we're fine, but we arrive in Auckland on Wednesday to catch up with my friend Michael, and we're hiring a car to come and stay with you in Waterworth sometime if that's okay?" he asked.

"That'll be lovely, what a wonderful surprise, I'll see you both when you arrive. Text me when you're on the way okay." She was eager, excited and curious.

"Will do mum, see you next week."

Jonah was relaxing in the lounge, listening intently with eyes watching, he queried her as she put the phone down. He had never had much to do with her son from the first marriage. Carl was never around while he was off flatting with his girlfriend in the South Island.

"That was Carl, they're flying up next Wednesday and want to catch up to talk about something." Mixed emotions rushed through her veins, he didn't sound sick, it could be he was thinking of moving up to the North Island. Relentless excitement, worry and curiosity would saturate her entire life until they arrived next week.

"That's good, you need to see each other more, especially now while you're not well," Jonah says.

Smiling, "I'm fine, I just missed you when you were gone and it upset me so I couldn't eat, but my appetite is back now."

Her skin was pale and she was grateful she had some tinted makeup to wear when they came next week, but it was not about her. Gemma wondered why they were coming up from Christchurch, it was a long way so it must be something important.

Sunday had a noticeable change in weather and the following few days confirmed a cooler week.

Autumn coloured leaves lay on the ground in the orchard as the fruit had finished and throughout the orchard leaves of a crispy golden yellow would crunch under foot. The plum and peach trees were showing bare branches and the temperature certainly required warmer clothing.

Monday, she put off phoning the doctor wanting to ignore it, but that afternoon Dr Truson phoned while she was out in the garden; he left a message saying he had made an appointment for her. Playing it back while sitting in the lounge.

"Mrs Frederick it's Dr Truson here, I'd like you to come and see me to discuss your test results, I've put it down for Friday 31st March at 1pm. Let me know if that time doesn't suit you."

Jonah folded his newspaper in half and lay it down across his knee with a concerned, hard set mouth he looked up at her when she put down the phone, her face blank.

"Everything okay love?" he asked.

"Yes, I have an appointment with the doctor on Friday. It's a nuisance to have to go in, I wish he just told me over the phone eh, it's only to get my blood test results," she grumbled.

"Do you want me to come? We could visit a café after if you like or a walk in a park," he suggested, his eyes following her.

"Oh no, I'll probably want to come straight home after waiting. There's always a wait." Faking a nonchalant smile. Concealing her worry over what the doctor might have to say.

"I hope it's before Carl and Sue visit, they'll probably come on the Saturday eh," thinking out loud. "It'll be good to get it off my mind and enjoy their visit." She concluded.

"There must be something to discuss with you." Jonah pondered looking uneasy. No more was said about her health when she didn't reply and the week progressed with her feeling fine.

Friday ultimately arrived; they were both aware that this afternoon was the doctor's appointment which had been prying on her mind. Gemma will be glad to get it over with before seeing Carl.

As predicted she sat and waited in the reception area for over half an hour before walking into the doctor's room, "Hello Mrs Frederick, thank you for coming in, there are a few things to discuss with you now that your blood test results are back."

Smiling and taking a seat, Gemma tightly clenched her hands in the lap of her best cotton skirt, her hair tightly wound up in a chignon and she had applied tinted makeup endeavouring to appear like a healthy person, she could feel the racing of her heartbeat as she waited to get the results, completely unprepared for bad news. How does someone prepare for bad news?

"Firstly, I needed to rule out that you don't have what your mother had. Acute Myeloid Leukaemia, not that it's hereditary but it's surprising how many times things reappear in other family members who live in the same environment. Having a blood test shows if you have too many lymphocytes, which effect the body's blood forming cells in bone marrow and your lymphatic system. Your paler is a concern as when you came in and sat down I was shocked to see how pale your skin is. I'm pleased to say you don't have leukaemia but you are very anaemic." He looked up from the results in front of him.

"Oh yes, I probably need to eat better but I was very upset by Jonah's burns and couldn't cook or face eating."

"We can give you iron medication to help until that improves. The dizziness started when your husband was lost at sea and you collapsed is that right? We can probably put that one occurrence down to extreme stress causing an anxiety attack when you would have been breathing quickly. But now months later I would have expected you to be well again, so I also tested your blood for glucose levels which shows that you have Hypoglycaemia," he went on to say.

"What's that?" nervously hesitant to ask.

"It's low blood sugar and a good diet should correct that as well," he explained.

"What about all the bruises I keep getting doctor?"

"Well, looking at your notes you're taking Arthritis medication that can dilate blood vessels and may cause Vertigo, that's dizziness and possibly increase the chances of irregular bruising as well."

"So what do I need to do?"

"I'm prescribing iron medication and recommend that you have three good meals a day with morning and afternoon tea to correct your sugar levels, we don't want to alter your Arthritis medication unless we have to." He reached forward across the desk handing her the prescription and the account to pay. "If the dizziness doesn't improve come back and see me, but give it a month and you should come right,"

"Okay, thank you doctor."

Breathing a sigh of relief she grabbed her handbag and made her escape, relieved she got into her car catching a large breath of air and slowing her heart rate. Reaching for the drink bottle full of cool water she had left in the car especially. Thank goodness we are going to have many more years together, she felt tired and her eyes misted over with relief. Driving home to Jonah with good news she did not want to stop at the chemist to get the prescription filled, that could wait. Gemma needed to get home for a cup of tea, longing to tell Jonah how much she loved him. Driving around the central magnolia in the driveway experiencing a sense of solace, she opened the car door impatient to give Jonah the good news. He appeared at the front door of their home and stood watching, wearing his emotionless face like a cloak.

"Everything okay?" he inquired with a sad voice.

"Yes, I'm okay," Gemma called out with a smile, "Let's have afternoon tea." The dizziness had returned.

He put the electric jug on to boil as she reached up to bring down the biscuit tin from the top cupboard, keeping in mind doctor's orders to eat a biscuit for afternoon tea.

Arms encircled her waist as he turned Gemma to face him, gentle pulling her in for a cuddle before looking into her beautiful eyes and giving her a lovely kiss. It was time to explain it all to Jonah while they cuddled up on the sofa together, his arm draped around the top of her shoulders while holding their hot drinks, he released a huge sigh, he was anxious as well. His soft lips pressed hers gently for a long tender kiss and his warm embrace spoke volumes about how lucky they were. Jonah was as important to Gemma as she was to him.

Once upon a time she held on tightly to her independence and solitude as a way of protection and not ever wanting to endure the pain and fear of what came with giving her heart to someone. She lost that battle when meeting Jonah, he quickly became like food for her soul, a necessity in her life and she in his. No matter what happens as they age, they will go through it together. Gemma knew that she would never have to go through trials alone, Jonah was every part of her, together forever.

Running his hand gently down one side of her face he searched deeply into her eyes, "I'm sorry you got sick because of my stupidity, I wasn't looking out for you I didn't think of what could happen to us, I'm so sorry," he said remorsefully.

Squeezing his arm, "It's okay, we got past it because you were determined to come home to me, so you sorted it all out. Besides, I'm going to be okay too." She whispered between heart warming kisses.

"If I cook up a big pot of the pasta and mince that you love, will you take us to the butterfly house next week?" Gemma asked while snuggling into him.

"That sounds like a great idea, it can be our celebration, but we better wait and see when Carl and Sue are leaving, they might stay for a few days. I want it to be our day out without having to share you. I must admit that I was worried about you because of how pale you look, and then when you couldn't dance I knew something was wrong because you love dancing." Smiling down at his precious wife held tightly in his arms.

"Well, no need to worry now," she giggled. "I'm fine or at least I will be after you're well. I don't know how long they will stay, probably only a few days. Carl said he would text when they're on the way up to Waterworth."

An early 7am rise for Gemma, with her being so excited to see them both arriving this brisk Saturday morning, weather was pleasant with just a light breeze promising the beginning of an okey day.

"I think I'll bake some biscuits and fill the tin for their stay."

"Sounds good, can we have chocolate chip?" Jonah asked.

Laughing, "They're my favourite too, everyone likes them so I'll make a double batch." Pulling the trays out and lining the ingredients up along the top of the bench she began. It was a welcoming break from gardening and speculating over why the sudden visit when it was not a public holiday. Two trays of piping hot biscuits brought with it a chocolatey aroma wafting around the kitchen at only 10.30am, her phone dings with a text message.

'On the way now', she read. 'See you in about an hour for lunch.' She rushed outside to relay the message to Jonah before bustling around the house in preparation for visitors, making sure the spare room was made up faultlessly for them.

Oh, they're on the way, butterflies did a twirl in her stomach as she tried to think of something else to take her mind off the visit. It could be a good time to catch up on old friends, so she phoned Lynda who she had kept in touch with after they left dancing, occasionally they both met up at a café. Lynda answered the phone and Gemma found out how she liked her newly completed house, before explaining how excited she was to have her son and his partner coming to stay. They chatted about the weather, how it had changed, it was a lot darker in the mornings and how the last of the roses were looking nice especially Gemma's favourite Aotearoa, which was a strongly perfumed pink, one sniff of the scent was enticing and never enough, it was divine. She explained her annuals were finished and she was going to get started on planting her winter vegetables next week.

Both women agreed over the need to get some broccoli in, because the men love to have that in the winter months with creamy cheese sauce poured all over it. They said their goodbyes and promised to meet up again soon.

It took great willpower not to rush outside upon hearing a small rental car pull up in the driveway, but Gemma's health told her to go slowly or she could embarrass herself by stumbling. The excitement had been building, following a couple of years of not seeing Carl. Getting out of the car, still tall and wiry, Gemma thought he could do with putting some weight on. Smiles and cuddles all round, it was good to see Sue again having only met once before, she appeared to be a little overweight, Carl visited alone last time when she couldn't get time off work.

They both looked well, Sue's beautiful short curly hair was possibly a natural curl, Gemma wasn't sure, the colour of a cream sandy beach looked natural for her skin.

Gemma's voice was breaking up in an odd crock, like she had the flu, it was the raw emotion and welling up as they greeted each other, her eyes glistening Gemma was thrilled to see Carl. Walking towards the house Jonah helped lift their bags out of the boot and they were shown the spare room to stay in, while Wilson bounded around full of energy, he obviously felt the vibe of excitement, leaping up to slurp Carl whom he remembered very well.

Carl looked intently at her, "Mum you don't look well and you've lost weight."

"I'm fine, I'll put the jug on, would you like a drink or a walk around after sitting in the car travelling?" she queried.

"Both, coffee outside will be good mum," Carl pitched in.

"Okay!" Gemma called back while arranging fresh chocolate chip biscuits onto her favourite bone China plate. Jonah and Carl were happy relaxing in outdoor armchairs undercover of the pergola while Sue arrived to help make and carry hers and Carl's coffee, Gemma carried two teas out to join the guys.

Turning from the bench with one in each hand Gemma stumbled for a minute, coming over dizzy she leaned on the countertop. Sue had gone on ahead and didn't see. She quickly grabbed the dish cloth to wipe up the little bit of spilt tea which swished onto the benchtop, slowly pulling herself together thinking it must be all the excitement. With everyone smiling and seated around the circular table Gemma quietly sank into a wooden deck chair.

Sitting quietly for a moment, she removed two biscuits from the plate being offered around by Jonah. "Thanks darling."

Sipping tea while munching she was dying to ask but didn't, they both looked well so that was good. Looking back and forth to each other, but saying nothing possibly needing time to relax first, she was curious. After ham salad for lunch, which Sue had helped her with chopping and carrying, they wondered around the orchard and down to the jetty.

"Have you been out fishing lately Jonah?" asked Carl.

"No, not since the accident." They exchanged smiles and an airy silence settled over them like a cool mist.

Sue and Gemma went to sit under a weeping willow tree on the soft lawn as the men stood gazing with something on their minds.

"Sue and I are getting married," Carl blurted out loudly as he turned to look back at them both.

"Really, oh that's lovely you've been together for a few years now, I'm sure at 36 years old you should know what you want. Is Sue about the same age?" Gemma asked.

"I'm 31 and we've been together for four years now," Sue piped up.

The momentous moment shared and the release was spread wide, although having received Gemma's approval Carl still looked weighted down, as he continued on to make another announcement.

He staunchly declared, "You're going to be a grandma." He waited and watched.

"Oh, congratulations again, lucky I'm sitting down." Everyone laughed and the news was out, the cloud dissipated and the atmosphere lightened into a celebration as any stress faded from their faces. They must have been worried about not being married and having to explain the baby.

"The baby's due in April." Sue smiled as she proudly touched her tummy.

She seemed incredibly happy about having a baby and went on to explain that they only wanted a few friends at the wedding, not a lot of expense, just food and music.

There was still something to discuss, and it all came rushing out, "We've been wanting to ask if we could have it here, because we only rent and there's not enough space. We came up to see Carl's friend, his groomsman is in Auckland and my bridesmaid lives in Christchurch. We're adamant that we don't want a big fuss." Sue explained, her face scrunched up, and her head sunken down in an anxious enquiring way.

Gemma glanced over at her husband; Jonah gave a little nod of approval.

"Jonah and I would be privileged to hold your wedding here. We were pleased with how our reception went, and it was intimate, genuine and worked really well. Didn't it darling?"

Jonah nodded.

Now they knew what the visit was about and the four of them were happy. The soft grass was relaxing and they all sat to look out over calming seas with soft ripples lashing the jetty as they chatted.

"We're also thinking of moving up to Auckland, so we will be closer to family. Sue doesn't have any mum or dad now, so it would be a great help for us to be near you both when the baby's born," Carl went on to explain.

"I'm going to be a grandma!" Gemma exclaimed loudly, "That's something I definitely didn't expect, I can't wait to tell your sister Bridget and John the good news."

Everyone laughed amidst light-hearted chatter, excitement filled the afternoon air along with many questions to ask Sue.

Eventually they all made their way back to the house for a cup of tea and biscuits. How wonderful to think they will move to Auckland; Gemma was over the moon.

The news had snowballed into better and better.

Chapter 16

Back in the kitchen getting clean mugs out again, "What about your work?" Gemma asked.

"Sue wants to continue with her hairdressing as long as she can stand, and I'll have to find something in construction up here," Carl said, about to sit down, the breakfast bar stool screeched on the polished floor.

"The house prices are high but we want to find a home to fix up and to hopefully increase the resell value, then move on to a bigger house later on. We can make do for now," explained Carl.

Jonah remained thoughtful, "You should find something, a lot of landlords are selling their rentals and cashing up. Insurance and mortgages are too high for setting a reasonable rent in Auckland, and it's proving to not make enough profit anymore for the landlord. You'll just have to look around."

Silence as minds were ticking, "Maybe an old batch on the windy west coast or a little bit out might become available," Gemma suggested. "That's good news about the wedding and the baby will have good babysitters, it will all work out." She smiled confidently.

Jonah walked over to pick up the phone, he began to order pizza because he observed how pale Gemma looked, she was getting tired.

"It's going to be a busy winter, and a really joyous spring with a new baby around." Gemma announced enthusiastically after all the wonderful news.

"We want to marry as soon as possible being as Sue is getting bigger by the day." Carl looked lovingly at Sue.

She smiled like she was carrying not just a baby but something quite special, and she wanted to look like a bride not an expectant mum at the wedding.

"Do you think we can arrange a small wedding of about 25 – 30 people here, for the 30th of November?" Sue looked with pleading eyes, currently appearing needy and vulnerable in her condition.

Hearing the high pitch of anxiety in her voice, Gemma was quick to reply, "If that's what my future daughter-in-law wants, then that's what we will make happen. Having it here is easy as wedding venues are often booked well ahead, and they're expensive."

Sue managed a nervous smile, it was understandably a lot for her to cope with, pregnancy hormones, wedding plans and leaving her home in another city. Having to face the world without her mum and dad, poor girl. Gemma didn't ask what happened to her parents but hoped to become good friends with Sue.

"I'll get a notebook for you to write a guest list, and tell me all the things you would like at your wedding and the colours you want in the flowers, we can go looking and try on wedding dresses if you like or would you like to go with your bridesmaid back in Christchurch?" Gemma asked.

"Oh, that would be great, I'd like you to help me, there will be a good choice in Auckland and I don't want to go on my own. My bridesmaid Annie might not have time to come with me, she works fulltime."

"We can have a look at ready made dresses in Auckland city and if you don't fall in love with one of them then you and Annie could sort one out in Christchurch. We may have to look at a lot of dresses before you find the right one."

"Hmm that's a good idea, a readymade one to try on would be quicker as well. We can only stay for the week, so I'll have to search online and try on in a day or so." Sue smiled.

The pizza arrives and the evening was spent discussing their plans for the future. Jonah and Gemma were both thrilled to be invited to play a bigger part in their lives, than what had happened in the past.

"Probably the best thing will be to have a good browse online tomorrow, we'll use my laptop to rule out styles very quickly. Have you got any must-have ideas? like necklines or full tulle skirt with layer upon layer to hide your growing tummy? Write down what you really want and we can search it up." Gemma suggested.

Sunday morning and the ladies couldn't wait to get started with the lap-top, settling at an old wooden work desk in the office after breakfast, they left the guys to do whatever.

"I found it so tiring driving here yesterday and giving you all the news, so I zonked out last night. But then I woke up early this morning all excited, all I can think about is finding my wedding dress and how to get the wedding organised," Sue rattled on and Gemma just smiled and listened.

An hour later with pad and pen in hand Sue had jotted down a few shops that had the style she was looking for, and they plan for a Wednesday outing after checking again to make sure the dresses were in stock, enquiring about the size, colour and fabric. They did as much as possible on the laptop. The rest of the day was spent scrolling around the real-estate advertisements before putting the device away so they could all head out for a walk through the Waterworth shopping centre.

Joyfully having a relaxed stroll along the water's edge that ran behind the shops before popping into a café for some afternoon tea.

Sleep came easily as the day drew to an end, issues had been sorted and discussed and a lot on their minds has been worked through. Sue was looking content and happy to be getting married; they had been together since she was 27 years old and her biological clock was ticking. She explained to Gemma that as a teenager she assumed marriage would be imminent for her, it was what she always wanted and expected it to be the norm, but life went on one day after the other with never a proposal until now, she's pregnant. Sue went on to say it gave them a wakeup call to be expecting a new little person who needed them to be responsible and grown up.

Her long-time friend and lover Carl had stepped up to face the fact he had been taking Sue for granted and the pregnancy had strengthened their resolve to stop drifting and settle down. Gemma could see their relationship was strong and it was time to get a home. She could see how much in love they were and was so pleased that they would be getting married.

Gemma was also thrilled to have them living closer so she could spend time getting to know Sue and be a grandma to her first grandchild. It had all come as a complete surprise, something new to look forward too, might be just what Jonah needed as well.

Monday morning the two were keen to start looking at the availability of the wedding gown styles Sue had jotted down as her preference.

"Did you sleep well?" Gemma asked them both in the kitchen making breakfast.

"Yes, we're so glad that we came to talk with you both. You have a lovely big place and there are motels close by for our guests to come and stay. I don't think many will come, my brother Tom and his wife Silvia live in South Auckland. That's who we had to visit before driving up here to see you both, they have one child I don't know if they'll bring her to the wedding or leave her with the grandparents. Carl's best friend from school is Michael, do you remember they went to college together? He has agreed to be groomsman and Waterworth is close enough for them to drive home after the wedding and reception." Sue explained.

"We can hire table and chairs for outside and incorporate the outdoor area as well with its roofing to sit under, I don't think we'll need a marquee, just an awning draped from the pergola roofing across to some poles in the ground." Carl piped in before standing.

The men left them to it, they went off and sat in the lounge to talk about what deposits and interest rates for buying a home were doing at the moment, somewhere around Auckland or close to Waterworth, because that offered the most job opportunities.

The two women sat comfortably at the desk in the office so as not to disturb the men in conversation. They surfed the internet for bridal boutiques, scrolling through the many designers online she ruled out anything tight, straight, low neck lines and white as she wanted something ivory, bone or an off white shade. An hour later they agreed that it had been time well spent as a lot of traipsing around had been avoided, by seeing what was in stock, narrowing the upcoming outing down to three stores they really wanted to look at. They were all in Auckland city or close to it and decided to discuss that with Jonah and Carl.

Carl suggested that he drive them all to town on Wednesday in the rental car, they could enjoy a look around the city while Gemma and Sue go dress shopping. Gemma emailed the three stores to advise them of the styles wanted to try on for Wednesday and fingers crossed they might find the right one.

"Thanks Gemma, it has been a huge help looking on your laptop as my legs get tired now if I walk around too many places." Sue explained.

After sending the emails, two replied. They will be expected and one replied that they would have other gowns that meet the requirements waiting to try on as well, they are the latest and not online as yet.

"The next thing to do, will be to get the invitations sent out to see how many guests we are expected to cater for." Gemma suggested a plan.

"Are the ready made invites with matching coloured envelopes nice do you think?" Sue queried, her eyes looking up.

"Yes, I've seen them in the stationary shops and they are really nice, or we can design one and have it printed on nice paper." Gemma suggested.

"No, I just want to go to a good stationary shop and buy some that I can write on personally. Time is an issue so let's get them sent out urgently," Sue said thoughtfully.

"A personal note will be appreciated by whoever receives them, what colour do you have in mind?"

"My bridesmaid Annabelle suggested apricot, she has ginger hair and likes to wear those colours."

"Apricot is nice and might be available in invitations and envelopes, so let's have a look on Wednesday if we have time. We need to match Annie's dress fabric to the cards as well."

"Yes, her mother offered to make the dress if I provide the fabric, she has a pattern and the groomsman and Carl can wear hired grey suits. If we don't find a tie with the apricot somewhere on it, then cream or ivory would be okay," advised Sue.

"That sounds lovely, the ties might be the most difficult to match but you can always get off white shades. It sounds like you have it all worked out, good for you." Pushing away from the laptop they both needed a stretch, so stood up pleased with the progress before going to get a cuppa.

"November 30th will have vibrant flower colours available, especially the marigold family, daisy's and apricot roses will be flourishing around that time. Marigold buttonholes for the guys with maidenhair fern and a sprig of Gypsophila would be beautiful." Gemma suggested.

Sue's head nodded enthusiastically in happy agreement. Planning was underway and they had a lot of shopping to do, but Sue knew what she wanted and they were all on the lookout.

Jonah would take Carl to view suits and ties at regular stores then Michael will be able to source the same suit in his size to try on.

They won't buy ties just yet, until after they have the invitations sorted and then they would decide on a good tie. They still needed to book a photographer and minister for the big day. She and Jonah had agreed to offer to let them move in with them until after the wedding, when they leave their rental accommodation and start going for job interviews. Everything was so difficult and busy so they wanted to make the move as easy as possible.

Jonah and she had decided to set conditions though and stated that they could only stay for three months. Not wanting to lose their freedom and hopefully after that time the couple would have found jobs and be able to move out. They would soon have a baby to care for and needed to be a settled little family.

Wednesday morning, everyone was up early to travel 45km to Auckland city, looking forward to a great day out shopping, they stopped on the way to choose ice-creams at Orewa beach. It was a relief to get out and stretch their legs, the girls chose Pecan and Caramel, which was sweet and nutty, while son Carl wanted to try the new citrus/pineapple ice-cream and Jonah seized the tried and true orange/chocolate chip ice-cream. After a brief stroll on the beach quietly slurping and licking to the sound of the sea gently lapping ashore, the seagulls stood longingly watching as the adults focused on not dripping any of the ice-cream now the morning sun was endeavouring to melt the precious treats.

With each day the weather was noticeably warming, as they edge closer to November with just a pleasant soft breeze and the frozen creaminess mingled with a whiff of salt air.

Sue resolved to sit under a tree and concentrate on her slurps until completely devoured. The others just stood around until the last of the cones were finished and Carl helped to pull her back onto her feet as they all made ready to set off once more.

It would only take another 35 minutes to get there and it was early, next stop would be Auckland city for lunch. Driving straight to the lower city underground carpark they did not even consider trying to find street parking as they had no idea how lengthy their shopping trip would be.

"There is a large department store over there so we'll have a look at the ties and take photos of anything we think is right. There is also a menswear retail store that hire out suits," said Jonah.

Carl intended to try on grey suits and book one for the 30th of November then Michael would come to town and match his.

"Okay, I'll turn my mobile on and we won't catch up with you two for a while, we have three bridal stores to view and we have fittings booked so that all takes time. Sue and I will get our own lunch in between shops, so you two should do that as well. See you later, have fun and we will meet back downtown by the boats okay, I'll text you." Gemma hastily explained to Jonah.

After a kiss with their partners off they went very excited, clutching a map Gemma had printed off before leaving home.

Arriving outside the first store exuberant to view wedding dresses, the shop front had very impressive huge, angled glass panels to create a bay window with a tall slim mannequin wearing a lavish and very expensive looking gown, it was jaw droppingly beautiful. Not white but an unusual pale caramel with sequins decorating a shimmering satin, full length with extended back draping along the floor of the display window.

"Oh wow, do you think I can afford anything in this store?" Sue looked forlornly at Gemma.

"Yes you can, I decided to check that online and with the amount you told me that you had both agreed to. The styles you like are usually made in less expensive fabric and have less embellishments so just have fun, don't worry, try on whatever you want and just enjoy today," she laughed reassuringly.

Gemma was enjoying the time with her future daughter-in-law and was sorry that her own mother was not there for Sue.

They walked up to the counter to advise that Sue had arrived for her appointment.

"Right this way, my name is Peggy," she said. "We've hung up the dresses you like and can also show you around the entire store to see if something catches your eye."

Shown through to an area that opened into a beautiful room with vibrant green plants in huge white pots, pastel coloured sofas were scattered around with several changing rooms off it.

Sue was relieved to sit for five minutes while Peggy rolled out a selection of stunning gowns all with pretty necklines, not slim line or tight, and as requested all of various shades of white or pastels. They were hanging from an intricately designed white painted wooden stand, on casters. Appropriate little cherubs with bows and arrows were carved along the top rail, everything was very elegant and expensive looking.

Sue looked over to Gemma and she smiled back, she wanted Sue to have this unique experience, hopefully it would be the only time she ever got married, it needed to be special. Pushing herself up off the couch Sue stood and slowly moved the coat hangers as she carefully scrutinized each gown along the rack. Every dress was so delicate and beautiful there was no arguing that fact, and it would be a difficult decision.

"What colour do you dislike?" Suggested Gemma, trying to reduce the number by ruling some out.

"This one here is too bright." So she pushed it to one end and kept looking.

"Do you want to try all of them? I can hand them to you." Gemma offered.

"Okay, I'll take a couple in with me." Carefully hanging two over the golden scroll hook on the changing room wall.

"This is scary, they're so beautiful," she whispered.

"I'll pass it over your head and you can slip it on," said Gemma.

The first one looked okay, the second one didn't hang right over her tummy, and as Gemma continued to remove each gown from the changing room she carefully replaced it with another one. Then Sue paused and took longer staring at the gown she was wearing.

"You look lovely." Gemma smiled.

"What a gorgeous colour, do you like it? she asked.
Just a subtle hint of grey in the palest shade. "Yes it's lovely, what do you think about the length though?" Gemma pointed out.

"Just ankle length is good; I don't want to trip over," she replied. "I love the short double frilled sleeves and the fabric is light and floaty which is comfortable for me to wear. The scalloped neckline is feminine don't you think?"

"Yes, it's very pretty, do you want to try on this last one?" Gemma asked holding it up for Sue to view.

"No, it's not as nice as this one I'm wearing so I won't bother. I really like this," Sue was all smiles.

"Shall I ask the shop to hold it for you; we can come back later after looking at other stores if you want to have a think about it?" Gemma suggested, making sure Sue was not being impulsive.

"Yes, that's a good idea, let's get something to eat to give me clarity." She laughed as she felt a bit tired.

Chapter 17

Peggy returned just as Sue came out of the changing room dressed in her own clothes and requested if they could hold the gown; the shop was more than happy to hang the dress out the back away from customers just for today only. So that gave them time to decide what to do. Upon leaving the shop, they looked along the footpath and saw a billboard café sign almost fallen into the road guttering, pointing it out to Sue before enthusiastically heading for that, it was not too far to walk for lunch.

"Thank goodness it's handy, I'm hungry and tired from trying on those gowns," she giggled as they walked. Bubbling over with chatter about the various laces used and laughing at the overly flouncy meringue shaped one.

After ordering paninis and coffee, grabbing the order number they headed for a round table at the back of the room, away from the traffic noise and fumes; a quick check of her cell phone it was 1pm so they had missed the café' rush, which was why only one elderly grey headed gent remained at another table.

It was an agreeable time to have a lively discussion over lunch; they still had two more stores to see if they wanted to. Sue rummaged in her stylish grey handbag and pulled out a photo that Gemma had printed of one gown she liked online. Gemma saying how she remembered liking the look of that one as well, it was not far away, just up a side street so they decided to investigate and not settle too early. Feeling that it was very important to try on everything before making such an important decision.

"Oh I forgot to look at the price of the one I liked!" Sue exclaimed, sounding anxious.

"I looked at the tag when I hung it up, it's a little bit more than you wanted to pay. Jonah and I are happy to contribute that extra to the wedding cost if you want that gown." Guided Gemma.

"Are you sure?"

"Yes, we talked about it last night and set an amount we can afford, so if that's the one you want we can get it today if you like."

"The skirt was loose enough not to need any altering if I get married in a few weeks." She pondered.

"That's right." Gemma nodded in agreement.

Happy to relax with the frothy coffees and hot Paninis when they arrived, Gemma took the opportunity to text Jonah with an update before heading in the direction of the side street. The bridal store not as lavish but the clothes were cheaper, they did not have the wow factor so she found she only tried on the one they admired online. It turned out to be a bit of a disappointment, pretty online and okay on the hanger, but not so nice when she tried it on.

"I can't get the other dress out of my mind; can we go and get the one we put on hold, what do you think?" she asked.

"Yes of course, it was the most beautiful of them all and has everything that you wanted, let's go and buy it," she smiled while getting out her mobile to text Jonah.

'We won't be long, will meet up in about half an hour.'

Excited, they hastily headed for the first bridal shop they went into this morning, the foot path was now streaming with pedestrian shoppers so they carefully manoeuvred a way through, arriving to see Peggy. She remembered them and rushed off to collect the gown.

Sue wrapped her arms around herself, smiling and so happy watching as Peggy carefully folded it up between layers of soft white tissue paper into a very large white box. Prominently sitting on the counter they both swipe their credit cards before Sue proudly collected the large box, holding it close to her body with a blushing smile spreading from ear to ear. It was a small price for Gemma to pay, participating in a once in a lifetime happiness, Sue was to be the beautiful bride her son would marry on a memorable day in their lives. A wonderful day they were all privileged to be part of, helping her to choose her wedding gown was overwhelming, and as they walked silently downtown Gemma hid her eyes from Sue, welling up with emotion, she had enjoyed the day. Walking swiftly towards downtown they found the guys sitting by the boats chatting.

They looked up as Sue shouted, "I found the one." Their eyes surveying the large white box with suspicion.

"Oh that's brilliant," said Jonah. "That was easy."

"No, not really, I lost count of how many dresses I tried on and how many I didn't like," she laughed happily.

"That's great. But before we leave, you need to look at a photo I took of ties." Jonah passed his phone to Gemma.

"Oh, they look very smart with two shades of grey and splashes of black and apricot, what do you think Sue, should we buy a couple for the men to wear?" She asked.

"Yes I like them, they should go with apricot fabric for Annabelle's dress, but what if we can't find invitations in that colour?" she queried.

"Well, I took the liberty of purchasing these apricot invitations and envelopes for you to view, I can return them if they're not right." Jonah reached into a paper bag he was carrying.

The invitations held beside the photo of the tie looked a perfect match. Very pleased the ladies looked around to find a vacant bench to sit and rest their feet while watching the receding tide, sending the men off to buy two ties. Sue carefully placed the important white box to one side of the seat and kept glancing at it to make sure she was not dreaming, and it was still there. Jonah and Carl didn't take long to return looking very pleased with themselves.

Job done, they all decided to head back to the carpark, relieved that it was fairly close, after having had a successful day shopping they were all in agreement, they were glad to go home.

The wedding was coming together and the four of them sat contentedly back in the rental car contemplating how things had changed in only a few days, and how well they all got on together.

Looking out to sea it was still calm, and strange to think that the sea had followed them to town. The tide was going out, just as they would soon be on their way home as well. Gemma's health had not been an issue all day she just felt a bit tired now. She was getting older and told herself it was to be expected. Sitting quietly beside each other, looking out of the car window she felt pleased for this young lady to be coming into their lives, with the potential to be a delightful new extended family going into the future.

A lovely day had come to an end, and arriving back to the lone Magnolia tree sitting majestically in the centre of the driveway, they all got out of the car and Sue carefully took her treasure to the bedroom, giving strict instructions that no one was to open the white box. She carefully laid it on top of the high chest of drawers.

Jonah caught up with Gemma in the bedroom as she tentatively told him about her lovely day and how much it had cost him on the credit card. Jonah smiled and nodded in acceptance. She didn't understand why she felt relieved to be home, but looking tired and pale it was a joint decision to have an easy mince pie, gravy and chips with green peas for tea. Jonah and Gemma eagerly put their feet up to relax and unwind in front of the television while the other two prepared it.

Unfortunately the count down began, with only two more days to enjoy all being together, it was important to return the hire car back by Saturday afternoon. After breakfast, the next morning Sue retrieved her list of possible guests and showed it to Carl to ask advice on anyone she may have unintentionally left off the list, anyway if they think of someone they can always send a late invitation. She settled down at the table after breakfast impatient to get the invitations personally written out, then slipped each one into apricot envelopes ready to post. Thinking that the sooner they received the replies back she would know for the catering, and how many chairs and tables to hire later on.

Jonah suggested they could get the same catering company 'Occasion Foods' to do the food as he and Gemma had at their wedding, it was excellent and they did have an extensive choice of menu for them to choose from.

Holding back emotions Sue began to speak "We have a list of 30 friends and a few family to invite, I'd really like my sister Brenda to come but she lives on the West Coast of the South Island so I'm not sure if she'll be able to make it. She's divorced, on her own and has two little school aged girls, so she'll find it expensive to come up here." Pausing with a sad look, the emotion glistening in her eyes.

"I'll get the invitations all written out today so we can post them on our way to return the rental car," she continued.

"While you do that, I'll look up photographers and jot them down for you to look online, have a look to see how good their photos are, get quotes and then you can book the best one." Gemma suggested, trying to keep the mood cheerful and not melancholy.

"We don't want a minister; we'd prefer to just pay a marriage celebrant," she looked into the air while thinking about it. "I can organize one from Christchurch when we get home." She continued thinking out loud.

"Yes, one should be able to email you a draft copy of a nice programme and arrange the document to be signed by your groomsman and bridesmaid when they witness the signatures. She'll just want all the information and their full names, it should only take a few days to design a programme of service and email you samples to fill in names, choose the colour and design preferred." Gemma explained.

"Yes, I'll find out, I don't think we need to meet until the wedding day, I can direct message if there are any questions. Confirmation of acceptance of the quote for the service and registering the marriage can be emailed I would think," Sue said.

"Look at her website she might have a video of her work." Carl uttered quietly while relaxing in an armchair within hearing distance.

"Later this afternoon we could visit our local florist, it's not far to go and discuss flowers, that way you get to know her before you go home. You could place an order for the 30 November 2023. Then that will be another thing sorted for you," Gemma piped in warily.

"Yes, that sounds like a good idea. You and I can do that before they close today."

Gemma was loath to leaving the house again, but her desire to help was strong as she prayed for strength, she understood that they did not have a lot of time left before the wedding and were running out of it. Keeping busy with organising and planning she had forgotten to pick up her prescription so while they were out she would do that as well. Fortunately, sleep came easily each night now cuddled into Jonah, and her appetite had returned with a vengeance. She had gained another kilo in weight since she had been cooking evening meals for a family. Gemma was thankful to not have had any dizzy spells for a few days now.

Life seemed to have taken the right path as Jonah also enjoyed Carls company, they talked mortgages and job opportunities. His laughter could be heard from the kitchen, Gemma smiled as she listened to his endeavour to mentor her son, encouraging Carl to apply for jobs by email while in Christchurch. Carl proudly explained they have been saving one wage for over two years now and have a good deposit saved, while Jonah advised how the bank would be pleased with the regular savings, but that they would both need a job to show that they can repay a loan.

Looking online and local newspapers for employment opportunities while the wedding details were finalised, they both plan to keep looking, and start applying for anything that comes available. Peeking from the kitchen Gemma's heart warmed, pleased to see Carl getting to know his stepfather better.

Saturday morning arrived and the mood was very sombre, after enjoying a great get together and a fantastic visit they had to say goodbye for now. After the surprises and life changing news it was sad to see them go, they hugged and waved goodbye in the driveway, remaining positive because they knew the pair would soon be back for the wedding. After watching until the car drove out of sight Jonah, Wilson and Gemma went for a walk around the orchard, making plans to go to the butterfly house not tomorrow on Sunday, but opting for a quite Monday when families were back at school and work.

The intricacies of family life were becoming overwhelming and more stressful than she could cope with for too long, putting it down to her time of life, although an enjoyable visit neither of them was prepared for it. Gemma just needed some quiet time with her husband sitting side by side watching the sun slip slowly away, changing from bright blue to dark as the day ended and they looked forward to tomorrow. After tea they sat comfortably in the lounge each reading a book, Jonah unable to focus on his and constantly looking out of the window.

"Jonah is something wrong or doesn't that book interest you?"

"I've been thinking about an advert I read when searching the paper with Carl, a voluntary handyman is needed to help in the local opportunity shop that helps fund an animal shelter," he explained.

"Oh, what did it say?" curiosity creeping in.

"They want someone to help with shelving and moving heavy things usually only 1-2 mornings a week. I think I might volunteer." He pondered.

"Really, would you like to do that?" she asked.

"Well, it would get me out and I need to do something worthwhile, something with a purpose now I'm retired." Jonah said.

"Ring them up, do you still have the number? I don't mind and I can go on my garden trips without you."

"Okay, I'll phone them." Pleased that he had talked it over with Gemma.

"It'll be closed today Sunday, why don't you just phone early in the morning before we go out, and enquire if you can pop in. The butterfly house is on the way?" She suggested smiling.

"Yes that might work, I would look forward to going to work again." He laughed before getting stuck into his book.

It was good to see him happy again, and she hoped the op shop would accept his offer of help. She understood how difficult it was to age, wanting to help people, keep using your brain and sharing a wealth of information learnt through to retirement age. Being useful, at the same time understanding that seniors can not work as hard as they used to in their younger days. Monday was a thrilling day to look forward to, and all thoughts of the kids moving and the wedding was put aside as they put their own plans into action. Much as they loved having them stay their lives took on an exciting new direction.

They would also need time to become accustomed to the idea of becoming grandparents when son and daughter-in-law live closer to home and they looked forward to the challenge.

Monday morning Madeleine answered the phone at the opportunity shop; after Jonah explained he had seen the advertisement in the paper requesting a volunteer and that he would like to be considered. The woman was elated that she might soon have someone.

"Oh that's wonderful, we are in great need of some help and it's all for a good cause."

Pleased, she agreed that Jonah could introduce himself when driving passed the shop later on in the day and promised to inform Keith, the manager about it. He was out at the moment but would be back, and he would decide on whether Jonah was the right person to help them. Jonah was asked to please bring his ID and drivers licence and would need to be capable of dealing with the public, she requested any character referees he might have as that would be helpful as well.

They had a quick lunch so they could get going, he and Gemma set off on the butterfly house outing intending to stop for the interview on the way. When he came across parking Jonah didn't worry about turning the car around and just parked on the left hand side of the road. That would make it easier for them later to just continue on their outing after speaking with Keith. With a self-confident stride and a steady pace he crossed the road with paperwork held firmly in his hand, while Gemma waited in the car.

The shop door was latched back to display a fresh interesting mix of paraphernalia all donated to help raise money to care for homeless animals at the dog rescue centre.

Fingers crossed they accept him to be a volunteer as it could be just the right project for Jonah. Half an hour passed before he reappeared, even looking from the parked car across the road Gemma could see his smile was so broad, it was plain to see all went well as he stood and watched for a break in the traffic.

Gemma watched on, praying that he would take care and pay attention crossing the busy highway while his head was in the clouds, he must stay vigilant and be careful. Rushing across from the other side of the road as soon as there was a break in the traffic he swung the car door open, quickly taking a seat before the lights turned green and traffic again filled the busy road.

"Yes I can start, Keith was very grateful to have me help and Madeleine, the lady I spoke to on the phone suggested Mondays, because they have a lot of sorting and arranging to do with new deliveries from the weekend. I said I could also do Thursday mornings as I know sometimes you have gardening trips out and that way you won't miss me," he scrambled to get it all out; he was so excited.

"That's wonderful Jonah, congratulations," she replied with a genuine smile, she was pleased for him. "I hope you'll like it."

"Me too," Jonah agreed nodding. "I haven't done any shop work before but I won't be on the counter, pretty much I will be on my own just moving and sorting. I think I will like helping and especially when the money made is for the animals." He beamed.

Chapter 18

At first, approaching the butterfly house it just looked like a warm glass house smelling of green fronds and musty soil. Apart from a trickling sound coming from water running over a placement of rocks it was tranquil and silent. They were fortunate to be alone in the house undisturbed, standing quietly to watch without disruption.

It was much like a small scale version of a grasslands and they spotted three different kinds of butterfly among many as they settled on their favourite plants. Gemma recognised the two metre high Buddleia tree covered in flower. Bright purple spires had a screen of butterflies nestling in every flower or lightly fluttering above each flower bracket, sometimes hovering and almost stationary, it was an awesome sight. Masses of regal orange/red Monarch with their distinctive white spots swoop around swan plants, searching the length of hanging lime green swanlike pods left swinging on bare branches, where the butterflies had devoured and completely stripped it off all the leaves.

Attractive lazy Emperor and the smaller common white butterfly fluttered and glided around in contented bliss. They were among a few of the species they recognised. While standing still the butterflies floated on air, unafraid, and one landed on Gemma's outstretched arm, Jonah quickly captured a photo with his mobile.

It was such an amazing phenomena when they flew on mass and landed, completely covering plants in wings of moving waves. Safe from predators or sprays and provided with the freedom and food to enjoy their short lives, it was undeniably magnificant.

In secret the heat was beginning to affect Gemma and was becoming unbearable, she became lightheaded, dizzy and began to waver a little, not telling Jonah she continually sipped from a cold water bottle, grateful they had remembered to fetch two of them from the car before locking up. They enjoyed the butterfly house and were glad to have seen such an extraordinary sight.

Passing through the exit gateway Gemma noticed an ice-cream van positioned alongside the carpark reserve. What a perfect place to park. She looked up at Jonah just as he looked down at her, they both laughed, not having to ask as they made a beeline to get an ice-cream before driving home.

Over the coming days emails flew back and forth, Michael the groomsman, had been to try on a suit and had happily booked the right size, twenty-six guests have advised they will be attending the wedding. Best of all, Sue's sister Brenda had her friend offer to mind the girls, so that was amazing news and everyone was thrilled she would be at the wedding. The bridesmaid Annabelle has taken her apricot coloured invitation to find a matching fabric and her dress was in the process of being made by her mum.

Everyone was bubbling with enthusiasm, pleased that it was all coming together and keeping with tradition the wedding service words were being kept top secret. Sue arranged the marriage celebrant without any help; it will be an enjoyable surprise for Gemma and Jonah to watch the couple get married and Gemma will need to tuck a handkerchief into her handbag to mop up joyful tears.

November arrived and days dropped off the calendar like petals off a spent flower all too quickly as they counted down, looking forward to Sue and Carl's big day, it was all planned and everything confirmed. Sue's bump had grown considerably, but she kept well and speaking on the phone sounded happy and excited to get the wedding over with before thinking about the baby's arrival.

Less than two weeks to go and Gemma offered the cottage for them to honeymoon in. She felt it to be important that they had that special time alone together just for a few days before returning to stay with them at the house. The plan was to drive up with as many possessions in the car as possible after arranging for large items to be packed and held in a storage container until they found the right home to buy. They won't need to bring much to the house as Gemma had everything set up for them in the spare room.

Now on their own Jonah, Gemma and Wilson decided to stay at the cottage for a weekend away together. Wilson leapt into the car very excited when he was informed they were going to the beach and to the park. They arrived to find the lawn needed mowing and everything needing to be tidied up, which was to be expected.

Gemma's intention was to put clean bed linen on the bed in preparation for the honeymoon couple, the bedroom smelt like freshly ironed crisp cotton, she placed perfumed soaps in the bathroom and a bottle of bubbly wine in the fridge for them, leaving a box of chocolates in the pantry as well with a little sticky note, 'Congratulations'.

Gemma lay still the next morning, waking up in her familiar cottage where she spent many years living alone, opening her eyes to recollect as a flash of emotions whoosh through her head, the times of loss and loneliness plus times of relief, feelings of safety and her love and gratitude of finding her furry companion. The building held a stronger spiritual understanding that she was never alone, God was always watching over her, guiding her forwards.

This place where Wilson grew up they both remember fondly, not only a tail wag but full on body wagging while happily running around in his yard, with the peaceful pastel colours of the cottage garden, the heavenly scent from the flowers filling the air and the huge feijoa tree. The tree he mastered the art of leaping up to shake the branches laden with fruit, he watched them swing in all directions, any that fell off, he picked up and bit in half, laying on the lawn before he began licking the inside and consuming the pulp. As a puppy he soon learnt the outer green didn't taste nice but just like an egg the inside was good. Watching him run around brought back fond memories. Although much treasured, she found she has never regretted leaving the cottage by the sea as her new life evolved to bring contentment and love. It was time to move on with her life, making room to share her future with a delightful man who became a big part of her life.

It took Gemma a couple of hours to have a good dust and vacuum around while Jonah mowed the lawn. Afterwards the warmth of the sun felt good to relax in. Picking up Wilson's lead it was time to proceed down the well-trodden path past the old houses and the clay bank where Gemma was once fascinated by the many holes carefully made to host seabirds nests. Everything looked the same, the house colours had faded and a couple of homes had new owners, obvious by the cars parked in the driveways and the new fences, but mostly it was the same.

She walked hand in hand with her husband, weirdly reminiscing and unable to walk past the salt and sand blasted park bench Wilson and she were so fond of, they sat there many times over the years to breathe in the tranquillity of fresh sea air, taking time to be mindful of the beautiful surroundings they now shared together with Wilson lying up against their legs.

Jonah exhaled, "Its amazingly quiet here."

"Yes, no traffic just the odd boat trailer. The tide swooshing in and a few locals, mostly retired people. A couple of them have a morning swim to keep fit, pretty brave I think as its too cold for me. It's a long way from workplaces for families to live here, but it's great for the retired."

"I can see why you liked it." Jonah nodded his head.

The roar of the waves supreme, with the cry of the sea birds chorus resonating over the violet and blue ruffled waves, and the fast moving tide pushing ashore, insistent on claiming more ground. They watched as nature measured this environment, unable to ignore the immensity of the universe looking out to sea, they sat together small and insignificant, being absorbed as one with sea, sky and land, the infinite universe.

The metal clasp clanged as Gemma bent to unclip the lead from his collar and all three continued on, into the reserve where

Wilson took his freedom. He bolted across the freshly mown park like an illusion of flight, his joyful expression of freedom as he appeared to leave the ground. She smiled, pleased for him.

Returning from the beach they settled into two comfy cane armchairs, more sheltered and away from the sea breeze, while Wilson took off around the cottage to find a toy to chew.

"Shall I get us some mixed nuts to munch on before getting tea. I was thinking I would just make a pizza, I brought tomatoes, onions, cheese and ham with us for the weekend, and there is still a jar of spicy sauce in the pantry," she chatted away.

"Yeah that would be nice, I'll open a bottle of wine."

He went to get two crystal flute glasses out of the kitchen cupboard where Gemma always left a couple of nice glasses at the cottage for them to use on holiday and then he collected the wine from the car.

Tipping the mixed nuts into a clear crystal dish Gemma returned outside to relax and Jonah appeared with the chilled wine he had in the car chilly bin.

Life was good, the two of them sipping and munching as they watched the pink sky turn to a dusky cerise and the light sank below the lush paddock hills in the distance.

Armchairs nestled beside each other. "You're deep in thought, is everything alright?" he asked.

"Yes I'm okey, sitting here together makes me melancholy," she said slowly, peacefully. "How lucky we were to have met each other, we're so fortunate." She smiled back at him.

"Yes," with a slight smile. "I'm sorry for getting lost in the boat and putting you through that though. I was the winner when you said yes."

Gemma reached her hand across to pat his arm, she nodded.

Jonah turned in his chair slightly. "You really haven't been your old self since the boat incident," he said looking at her seriously.

Their eyes met and she caught the worry concealed in Jonahs face and felt the solid connection they had together.

"I haven't said anything but I still get dizzy off and on, just out of the blue really. Even though I've put on weight I just don't seem to be getting better, somethings not right," she said quietly looking down at her hands clasped in her lap.

"Maybe go back to the doctor love."

"I think I might, even thought there isn't anything else wrong, it's just the light-headedness that's a bit awful."

"Phone up on Monday don't let it go on." Jonah said watching her.

"I will make an appointment as we have a busy time ahead." Gemma nodded in agreement, munched on the mixed nuts and sipping the cool sweetness of the wine.

"We have the wedding on the 30th of November and family to stay, then Christmas is just around the corner." He acknowledged.

They continued to sit and watch the beautiful sky as the end of another day together finished, before returning to the kitchen to roll out pastry and put together pizza for tea. They looked forward to the coming events and although they would always remember the lonely winter trauma of the boat capsizing, they tried to push it away into the past, pleased that Jonah had made a good recovery.

Spring has always played an important part in their lives, they continue to walk around the orchard observing the blossoms turn into fruit and enjoying the fresh new growth on the trees, life was amazing and if Gemma is well enough they want to start dancing again in the new year. Jonah kept encouraging her to take up writing when he volunteered at the shop as he enjoys editing and discussing it.

There was plenty to do in the garden to get it ready for the wedding and then Christmas, they both enjoyed the weeding out anything that had finished blooming and trimming off spent flowers, cutting back unruly new growth that was in the wrong place and they were both so happy to be able to help Carl and Sue, it kept them busy having family move in until the couple found a home.

After a lovely weekend away together they packed the car leaving the cottage looking clean and tidy, Jonah may have to mow the lawn again before the wedding on the 30th but everything else was left perfect for the honeymoon.

Monday morning Jonah brought her a cuppa in bed.

"Don't get up, I'm off to the opportunity shop to help out. I should be home soon after lunch. Madeleine text me saying she only needs me in the morning as there's not much re-organising to do until the end of the month." Hesitant about leaving her, "Why don't you use the time to write a story? I'll edit it for you, and don't forget to phone the doctor for an appointment." He kissed her on the cheek as she sat up to carefully take the cup.

"Oh thanks, have a nice time," she called as he started to leave.

Wilson came running into the bedroom, Jonah had let him outside before going off in the car, so Gemma quickly drank the tea and started to get up. She had the doctor on her mind and was anxious about getting an appointment, hoping it wouldn't be a long wait.

It was only 8.30am so she phoned the surgery and was lucky enough to get a cancellation, (if she could come straight away). She leapt at the chance. Gemma wasn't sure whether to be concerned about dizziness or not, she didn't have any other symptoms and apart from when it came on, she felt quiet well.

Walking in she could see her usual Dr Truson, which was reassuring, someone she knew and who had known her for six years was great to put her at ease.

Gemma said the usual greeting and explained that the dizziness had not gone away.

"Yes I see that you have been here about it before, because you have had this problem for a while now I'm going to refer you for an MRI to check there are no problems, I'll also request a CT scan of your brain. We may not need it but we can always cancel it later if we don't, it just pays to apply now as there could be a wait. I also want to repeat the blood tests although everything was good last time we checked."

"When does it seem to bother you the most?" asked Dr Truson. "Do you notice when the dizziness comes on?"

"It doesn't seem to happen any particular time or place, sometimes just standing in the kitchen. I feel unbalanced, lightheaded. Sometimes flashing lights at a dance effect me visually and my eyes feel like they shake." Gemma blurted out.

"Hmm." Dr Truson wondered and tapped away on his computer, recording any information that might be helpful later on to find a diagnosis.

"How is your husband these days? Has he been out in the boat lately?" he asked in an attempt to make casual conversation.

"He's well, no he doesn't bother with the boat now, I doubt he will ever want to venture out to sea alone again," she said.

"Well that's done, you'll get an email from the hospital for your tests and I'll see you later on." He stood up to open the door for her.

"Thanks doctor."

Gemma slid into the drivers seat of the steely blue Corolla car Jonah had bought for her last year, when they decided her little Honda had become too old and untrustworthy. It was only a short drive home from the shops to arrive safely at their beautiful home they shared, and she wanted Jonah. He would still be busy until this afternoon and she noticed his absence. How strange, she thought she had kept her independence and yet a deep hunger inside longed to be with him.

Turning into the driveway she drove the short length towards the grand Magnolia she loved with the garden they planted around it. She smiled remembering when they found this place together, it was an instant success, they both knew it was perfect for them. The water, jetty and large lawn for Wilson to run around, a garden for Gemma and what a surprise at the end of the path best of all was the orchard. She smiled remembering, her lungs filled with tranquil air and her heart swelled with love, she was so lucky they had found each other and she felt positive everything would be okey with her health, she never wanted to be unwell for Jonah.

She entered the house and headed out the back door to see Wilson. "Wilson, here I am."

He came running. She mussed his fur with her hand as he woofed a greeting, before bending over wrapping her arms around his tummy for a big cuddle and he gave a sneaky little slurp on her cheek before heading inside to the kitchen.

Making a corned beef and pickle sandwich with a nice hot cup of tea she took them over to the window where she could view the tide rolling in to meet the grassy bank of the back lawn. The time passed slowly, until she seized her book to immerse herself in.

The jingle of keys turning in the front door and the joyous ring of Jonahs voice alerted her he was home.

"Hi love, I'm back." Smiling and happy he had enjoyed helping out and meeting the customers at the shop.

He found her with a book on her lap and pleased to see him. Bending over to kiss her as she stood to greet him for a long hug.

"I managed to get to see the doctor this morning," she explained.

"How did it go?" Jonah queried with a dark look.

"Okey, I need to have an MRI, CT and blood tests done."

"Oh, well that looks like he's doing a good job checking everything, you'll soon be right." His hand rubbed her back.

"I just have to wait for the hospital appointments. Did you have a good morning?" Gemma asked as she started to sit down again.

"Yes," he replied as he strolled over to get coffee and a sandwich. They then decided to take it outside for a walk around the garden with Wilson following along before he ran off around the orchard.

The two of them chatted over what they want to do next in the garden and were pleased with how fast everything was growing they talked about plans for future plantings.

Chapter 19

The deep warmth of the morning sun penetrated her bare arms as she sat luxuriating with her coffee outside, enjoying the glorious weather. Gemma despaired at the end of spring coming and facing the onslaught of a hot summer in the garden; they both appreciated a good growing season with plenty of rain to keep the garden plants happy.

Jonah was still hanging out in the shower at 7.30am which was still early for a retired person with not a lot to do today, just a bit of weeding and clearing around the garden, a wheelbarrow or two of mulch tossed around to top it off and to add protection from the onslaught of a hot dry summer approaching. Jonah liked to pile the mulch around and Gemma appreciated the well groomed look it created, while also being of huge benefit to the plants.

Her mobile shuddered along the glass top table as it rang. That's early she thought, I wonder who is ringing me now. It had just gone 8am.

"Hello, Gemma speaking."

"Sorry to phone you so early Mrs Frederick it's the appointment clinic at St Martins hospital. We have a cancellation by a patient who can't attend for his MRI, your doctor has requested an urgent test for you so would you be able to come in later this afternoon? otherwise it could be a few weeks away."

"Oh, St Martins is not too far from here and I'm not busy today, so yes! I can take todays appointment what time is it for?"

"It's for 2pm, I'm sorry it's short notice," she said.

"That's okey." Gemma spoke although a little flustered.

"Just give the information desk your name when you arrive, and she will tell you where to go, thanks Mrs Frederick."

"Okey bye."

Jonah had come out carrying toast and coffee, she explained to him that she was going out this afternoon, a change of plan.

"It'll be good to get one test out of the way and we can still enjoy a couple of hours together in the garden this morning." He smiled and gave a comforting pat on her shoulder as he sat down.

"Yes , its good to stay on top of things, I'll probably be gone most of the afternoon. Do you think you'll carry on mulching the garden , a good layer under the trees will keep it tidy for months."

"Yes, but we'll probably get it finished before you go out, I'll just add as much as I feel like and have a beer later with Stephan."

"Good idea." She smiled, not wanting to spoil his day. Her peace in the garden was tarred a little with the appointment blurring her mind.

However, when she arrived in front of the information desk everything became routine, she was jostled around to wait in a small area until her name was called. The test was painless and quick, not a problem. She said a silent prayer that the result wouldn't be a problem either.

The drive home was easy and she relaxed as she pulled into the driveway they planted together. Jonah was sitting alone when she ventured outside to find him and Wilson ran over with his greeting. Jonah's obvious pleasure to see her showed in his glorious smile, she glimpsed a deepening mixture of emotional heaviness, and wrinkles along his brow flashed a look of worry he tried to conceal. He stood up when he saw Gemma, reaching for her he pulled her into his arms.

"How did it go?"

"Okey. Just another one of those things we have to go through I guess." She buried herself against his chest and enjoyed the snuggly comfort, breathing in cologne that was him, she was home.

Looking deeply into his gorgeous dark eyes his mouth found hers for a long wet kiss.

"I'll be okey," she whispered.

A few days later they welcomed Carl and Sue who moved into the spare room, the wedding about to take place in two days time.

Guests who were attending and her sister Brenda were all staying at the local motel. It was nice that they all got to meet and breakfast together. Sue's designer dress had been hanging in the wardrobe for a week now to let any wrinkles drop out and she had her hair layered by her favourite hairdresser while still in Christchurch, so she was ready and very excited.

She and Carl finally went to meet the celebrant and spend time welcoming the bridesmaid Annabelle and all of the guests staying at the motel. It was the first time Sue had seen the bridesmaid's dress. She followed Annabelle to the bedroom waiting while she opened the wardrobe door, Sue stood in front of a soft apricot silk that shimmered and fluttered with the slightest movement, it was stunning, and she was pleased that Annebelle would be able to wear it many times in the future for special occasions. The dress was ready to take to Gemma's for the wedding on Saturday 30th and Carl would be with his groomsman at the motel, to later arrive for the 10am wedding back at the house. Everything was arranged, falling into place without any issues. A courier arrived on Friday morning with Sue's bouquet of daisies and roses and bright marigold buttonholes for the men, absolutely stunning and beautifully laid in a box which was allocated a whole shelf to themselves in the fridge overnight.

The caterer had set up and had it all under control with a refrigerated van, Jonah and Carl set out the tables and chairs late Friday evening and the caterer draped them beautifully on Saturday morning. The whole atmosphere was buzzing with activity and a hum of high spirits.

Gemma received a text message on Friday, *'No problem found in MRI' we will go ahead with a CT scan. Dr Truson.*

She quickly showed it to Jonah in private, he nodded and smiled. All she wanted to think about this weekend was the special time with family and friends enjoying a joyous wedding with her son, she expected Bridget to arrive for her brothers wedding at 10am.

It was a small gathering at home like Sue had requested. A well organised and relaxing atmosphere everything went off really well, and even though the weather couldn't be ordered they were presented with a lovely calm morning, the tablecloths and flowers stayed in place. Gemma had placed clip-on weights to the corners of each tablecloth just in case, and it was fortunate that the orchard trees were fully covered in leaves and small orange fruit forming complemented with colour, shelter and shade.

After the wedding ceremony, countless lovely photos were captured by Stephan who had offered to do so, he meandered around capturing every moment for posterity. Carl and Sue Gibson walked hand in hand back to the house while guests settled together at any table they chose.

It was a buffet lunch and long trestle tables set off to one side had been laid for after the speeches, meanwhile the newlyweds were freshening up for fifteen minutes back at the house, before making their entrance after everyone was seated.

It was beautiful and couldn't have been nicer. The speeches were short and sensible, thanking everyone for coming and for the elegantly wrapped gifts that had been mounting up on a separate table. The caterers brought out a wide variety of delicious hot and cold food to be set out for all to help themselves. It was a delightful celebration and Jonah had set up tranquil background music.

Gemma looked over at him as he turned it on to play, while everyone filled wine glasses and helped themselves to a delicious lunch her heart swelled and her face flushed with affection, she was so grateful to have him as her husband. They sat and ate while

Gemma continued to watch the contented happy faces of family and friends and was pleased that it had been a successful wedding day, she was especially warmed that it had been held at her and Jonah's home.

Pausing to take note that she had become dizzy with the looking around and decided to disappear back into the house for a little while, there was no way she wanted to fall over in front of all these people. Sitting inside she was able to listen to the happy sound of chatter, laughing and conversation coming through the open ranch slider from her armchair, before returning to say goodbye to them all.

The happy couple gathered at their car where they had already stashed bags into the boot, and everyone waved goodbye, waving and loud cheering sounded as they drove off to Gemma's cottage for a wonderful week of seaside honeymoon.

After the hum of voices dissipated and the familiar hush ruled once more, the guests slowly returned to the motel to collect their belongings and gradually everyone returned to their own homes.

Jonah and Gemma looked at each other breathing a sigh of relief and contentment followed by tiredness they cuddled together.

"Time for a cup of tea love?" he asked.

"Yes please," she said, heading off to put her feet up on a black leather footstool.

Cherishing the quiet they sat. "Well we have a few loads of dishes to put through the dishwasher before returning everything to the caterers tomorrow," he sighed.

"Yes, it won't take long, and the hire people are picking up the tables and chairs tomorrow, we only need to stack them," Gemma agreed with a nod of her head as she sipped on her herbal tea. "It was a lovely wedding, thanks Jonah for helping to achieve that for them."

"Your welcome love, it was a combined effort, now lets hope our house guests can find a job and a home to buy." He shrugged his shoulders in uncertainty.

"They do have a good deposit saved. It's just getting a job. Lucky we have the place to ourselves for the week eh!" She laughed and let out a loud sigh as she relaxed contentedly.

She noticed Jonah's raised eyebrow, a twinkle in his eye at the thought of having her all to himself for a while.

Their alone time together was tranquil after all the organizing and stress of wanting to provide the absolutely best wedding they could for family. They quickly settled back into their routine, Jonah went to the shop on Monday morning and was home to enjoy lunch with Gemma, and she found she rather enjoyed having the house to herself getting housework done and catching up on reading a book she had borrowed from the library. She had also arranged to have a catch up with her friend Lynda next week, from the Friday dancing. Gemma planned to use her time alone to keep in touch with people.

A solitary envelope with St Martins printed on the corner was lying in the bottom of the cold metal letterbox when she went to check for mail, opening the flap-down door she glowed at how much she liked to receive a letter delivered in the box instead of always online. While at the same time dubious from the realization, she slowly picked it up between thumb and index finger, she knew it would be an appointment date without even opening it.

"Oh well Wilson, lets see what it says."

The letter was brief and precise, she need not reply unless she couldn't make the CT scan appointment in two weeks time.

Sitting down she set the letter on the coffee table. "Only two weeks to wait, that's not too bad is it Wilson."

She bent to pat his soft golden fur and tickle behind his ear, Wilson responded by stretching and tilting his head to one side with a peaceful groan of appreciation.

Gemma was startled out of her worry and thoughts, she looked up when she heard the creak of the garage door lifting as Jonah parked his car in the garage, his long strides brought him closer to her for a quick peck on the check.

"Have you been okey while I was away love?"

"Yes enjoying myself, was it busy in the shop?" she asked.

"No just steady, I like chatting to the customers. Most of them have a cat or dog that's why they support the shop. They like telling me what mischief their pets get up to," he chuckled as she went to get lunch. "Oh you got the appointment quickly." He noted the letter open on the table.

"Yes, that's good isn't it." Gemma agreed.

Over lunch they discussed whether to go dancing this Friday, there was a new dance on that Jonah would love to check out, Gemma agreed she wanted to go as well, she would be careful.

As was usually the case they arrived early at the dance, this was a hall they hadn't been to before and they were both keen to see. The three piece band and the attractive blonde singer had only just started on their first song, so there were plenty of tables to choose from. Gemma chose a long wooden table with seating for six, it was away from the blast of the speaker further to the back of the hall, while Jonah went to buy a bottle of bubbly. Sitting, she looked around observing the lighting, which was dimmed with decorative battery powered candles also lit in the centre of each table.

"This is magical." Gemma announced on his return, the windows down one side of the room opened out onto the sea foreshore reflecting the fairy lighting strung outside under the rafters of an outdoor seating area, reflections flickering and bouncing off the water.

"Yes it is, it can't not be when you are with the right person".

She felt her face blush; colour tinted her cheeks with a warm rush as he gazed into her eyes.

"Shall we dance?" he asked, offering a hand.

Gemma was mesmerised as she took his hand, walking onto the polished dance floor he embraced her firmly and she felt safe. Melting into him, the romantic music started off slowly for the evening with rousing love songs. In the softly lit room they drifted all alone on the floor, hushed sultrily this was their first dance in months as Gemma had felt unsteady and embarrassed about her giddy head, she hoped no one would notice. Jonah held her tightly and they glided around the dance floor oblivious to others arriving. This was the last night before the newly-weds arrived back from their honeymoon, unaware of Gemma's health, which was something only Jonah knew about.

Sue and Carl's tired old car pulled up in the driveway and Jonah went to put the jug on for a cuppa.

They were all smiles, energetically chatting away about how much they loved being able to walk on the beach in the morning sunrise, and sometimes they ventured down to the beach for a stroll after tea. They also commented how pleased they were with how the wedding had gone, saying it was amazing and everything they wanted. Gemma remembered how that felt and was pleased for them to have enjoyed the time at the cottage, she cooked a lovely roast chicken dinner to welcome them back and by the following week they had settled in okay and were helping out with the cost of shopping. Sometimes they cooked one of their favourite meals to share, which was fun to compare different tastes and Gemma really enjoyed their company.

Carl and Sue both went hard-out to find work, going out most days in search of employment agencies to leave their details or sometimes attending an interview. It had only been three weeks before they both secured jobs, which everyone was pleased about. Sue was thrilled with getting short hours of standing while she was pregnant cutting hair, and Carl was all set with a full time construction position working for a housing company who had plenty of work on.

He complained to Jonah that it didn't pay well, but it would do for now while he kept looking for something else.

Gemma attended her CT scan and blood tests without any difficulty and was expecting to see Dr Truson the following Wednesday for the results. Her health had not changed which in one way was a blessing that it didn't seem to be getting any worse, but it was not getting any better either.

Jonah continued to volunteer at the shop, rushing out in the car enthusiastically every Monday morning. He was enjoying finding a place for everything, sometimes needing to put up shelving which he also enjoyed doing, a bit of carpentry added variety and he liked to help. He was also improving a flair for pairing different colours together which he had never thought about before, discovering what looked nice and what did not, and how to portray the furniture, antiques and treasures in their best light. He did like helping but probably most of all he enjoyed the socializing and chatting, he was getting to know the regular customers who browsed and asked him for help, like if he had any old picture frames in the shop to fit their dog photos. One old lady loved to collect fine bone China cups with roses on them and another collected salt and pepper sets.

Jonah liked the curious variety of customers that ventured in for a look, almost as much as what the shop sold. He would arrive home to tell Gemma all about them. A couple of times he went on both Monday and Thursday but that was unusual.

When Wednesday finally came around Gemma had found that waiting for results had been filled with sleepless nights, so arriving at the doctor's surgery was liberating, she awoke to a day pleasant enough morning as she took a seat after advising reception she had arrived; it wasn't a long wait before the nurse called, "Mrs Frederick."

"Yes." She stood up carefully to follow, prompting herself to never rush out of her seat anymore, as she wants to now grow old gracefully rather than having a fall.

"Have a seat Gemma, well we have your results back," he looked at her. "Good and bad news I'm afraid," he said in a matter of fact way with a completely expressionless face.

"Oh." She replied quite speechless and awaiting bad news.

"Yes, all of your results and scans have come back normal or unable to identify any problem. I had your glucose level checked as well and that's all good. So it would appear that you are having a mismatched pathway from your eyes to your brain, that is why sometimes you get a sensation of self movement when you are standing still or with normal head movement. It is to do with ear anatomy and is a type of vertigo or 'persistent postural perceptual dizziness.'

It can be triggered by changes in head position and sometimes visual patterns such as ocean movement or wavy patterns, your eyes are sending funny messages to your brain. You said how you experience light headedness from flashing lights. That can be a processing difficulty for your mind to deal with.

"Oh, what should I do then?" she asked.

"The bad news is, we can't do much about it, there is a clinic that uses exercises to try and rehabilitate or reset the body to stimuli if you would like to try that," he continued on. "You appear to have gotten vertigo after the stress of the storm your husband was in. It is possible nature will sort it out for you in time, now you have your strength back your body may go back to how you were before the stress of Jonah missing at sea, and the hours you spent watching the waves. You have been through quite a shock with his healing as well."

Tears began filling her eyes, she had been secretly withholding a fear of being seriously ill, relief flooded through her veins. Determined that she would learn to cope with the dreadful dizziness, she was okey and could live to be with Jonah for a long time to come, thrilled she managed a tired smile.

"Thank you Dr Truson for doing all the tests, I feel sure that I'll be okey and I won't worry about rehabilitation therapy. In time it will go away on its own."

Standing up slowly, she continued to look forward, not shaking her head too abruptly she turned slowly.

She would learn to cope with the inconvenience until it went away, certain that she would one day be back to normal.

A humble tide of relief engulfed Gemma as she raced back to the safety of her familiar car. She lay her head back in her car seat to allow any movement to subside, feeling so relieved, the first thing she wanted to do was reach for her mobile to text Jonah she was okey.

He replied with a text message, a big smiley face and a bunch of flowers to her phone, bringing a heartwarming smile to her own weary face.

Continuing to drive the few streets over a short distance, random houses flickered past her side vision, her mind went over all the days that she had sat at the window watching, waiting for Jonah's return when he was lost at sea. She recalled the small amount of food she was able to eat and thought back to having nights of no sleep at all while listening to the sound of waves splashing ashore and being haunted by the knowledge and fear Jonah was still out there, constantly revolved around in her head.

Gemma felt comforted that with today being a Wednesday, her husband would be at home waiting for her return while the other two were both at work, she ached for the private time to talk and she couldn't wait to see him.

The last few months of distress they endured together, both of them had remained positive, they had kept busy with the wedding plans while they maintained hope that the dizzy spells would go away. Jonah had obviously not wanted to face any health issues with the love of his life now that he had finally found her, and Gemma refused to imagine anything could go wrong now her life was finally on track.

Chapter 20

On hearing the garage door screech open and clunk down, Jonah stood up with a start from his chair. Once the car was safely parked he sped towards Gemma, pulling the car door open and taking her in his arms.

He held her tightly waiting anxiously to discover the answers to what was wrong with his precious Gemma, not wanting to let go of her.

"Its okey love, I'm okey!" she cried out. Cuddled closely, protectively into his chest. Her eyes looking up towards his as they began to fill with tears, he guided her towards to sofa.

"I thought I might have had something growing in my head," she broke down sobbing, quickly brushing the tears away as she blurted it all out. Looking up at him. "All the tests prove that I'm okey." Gemma breathed a sigh of relief.

"Do you need a drink? Tell me what the doctor said."

"He explained that I have vertigo which is not dangerous and it was probably caused by my constant looking at the waves when I was stressed, also flashing lights at dancing. My brain is just taking time to adjust to what I see. It might come right with time and I'll have to avoid confusing weird flashing lights and not sit for days looking at the movement of the sea," she explained.

Jonah sat with his arm around her shoulders. "I was afraid and just had to keep busy, I couldn't face you being sick. I never want to lose you," Jonah confessed as he self-consciously looked down at the floor.

"We can get back to normal now, without any distress or worry, we're so lucky to have each other," she smiled.

"Shall we have a walk around the orchard?" he fidgeted.

Jonah was unable to deal with the wanting to please her heart and soul, after so much hidden concern it was difficult to adapt to the relief of having her home again. They walked hand in hand.

"Everything is looking good, plenty of fruit to feed all four of us, especially the peaches, the trees are so loaded that I had to tie some of the branches up to the trunk to prevent them from breaking," he kept prattling on making conversation.

She stopped him speaking, wiped the tears from her face while looking into his eyes, his sensual aftershave she had bought him permeated the air. She knew she didn't want a walk around the orchard and was so thankful to be home with him alone and well. The relief was overwhelming and she wanted him.

Reaching up she put both hands around the back of his head, her fingers threading through the now grey thinning hair, she loved him and she desired him. She couldn't imagine Jonah not being in her life and she never wanted to lose him.

Jonah had won her heart all those years ago, they had gone through being separated by the storm capsizing the boat, however the sea couldn't win. His resolve to be together had overcome his demise and now the threat of her illness pursuing them was also unsuccessful. They were together and neither could imagine life without the other. Jonah gently squeezed her hand in his, he leaned in for a long sensual kiss before leading her to the bedroom.

Life continued on at a fast rate with work, whilst Gemma maintained the home and provided them all with meals. Three months later Sue's pregnancy was now taking centre stage; she kept well but needed to spend a lot of time with her feet up on a foot stool when she arrived home from work. The four of them were relaxing and happily lounging around outside in the garden enjoying a beautiful Sunday afternoon, when suddenly Gemma noticed that Carl and Sue kept glancing suspiciously at each other and appeared to be quelling a smile.

"What's going on with you two lovebirds?" she asked. After catching the secretive smiles.

"Well we might as well tell you," Carl spoke slowly. We have been to the bank and they have reserved a mortgage for us."

"Oh wow, that's wonderful news."

"We didn't want to tell you yet as we have made an offer on a little two bedroom house and wanted to surprise you," he continued.

"That's wonderful, Jonah sat upright, do you think you have a chance of getting the house?"

"Yes, it needs work doing to it and the agent said that is putting buyers off."

"Would you be able to restore it yourself?" asked Jonah.

"No problem, it's quite sound, in need of a new kitchen which we will need to save for later on, but it is a do up, needs painting inside and out. We like that it has aluminium windows and a single garage. A basic timber home that needs work, nothing special but a great start for us."

"I hope you get it. Is it far away from here?" asked Gemma.

"No that's the great thing, it's only a few streets away," Sue smiled. "I might even be able to push the pram here."

"Oh that would be lovely, fingers crossed that you get it." Gemma's eyes lit up and her heart did a flip at the thought of a grandchild just down the road, which would be incredibly perfect.

They didn't receive the call until late Monday evening and by then they were thinking that perhaps it was too good to be true. Carl read the caller display when his phone rang.

"It's the agent," he mumbled nervously to anyone who was around.

"Hello, Carl Gibson speaking."

"Congratulations! It's your agent Janet, and your offer has been accepted on No. 104 Bradshaw Road," she said.

"Oh wow, thank you that's great, and are they happy for us to move in soon?" he asked all excited.

"Yes because it is their holiday home sitting empty, once the lawyers complete the documents the handover can proceed. I have your lawyer details, let them know to proceed with the purchase and I will email the title information and get the keys through to them. Thank you for your business and good luck in your new home," she said beaming.

Sue was watching, excited she could see and hear what was happening and knew that they had bought a house. She was bubbling over with delight all keen to set everything up for the arrival of their baby in April. Everyone was standing around silently listening. Carl was also lit up with excitement as he hung up.

"We got the house!" his face displayed the intense exuberance that they all felt.

"That is wonderful news, congratulations you two." Jonah said and smiled while Gemma rushed over to hug them both.

This was their first home as they had always rented before, and now they were both so pleased that they had made the move. All the saving and hard work to get ahead had come to fruition.

"Oh my goodness! my grandchild will be living just down the road, that's unbelievable," Gemma cried out leaping in the air.

They all laughed, it was a wonderful outcome to prepare and get settled ready for the baby's arrival in April. The house was alive with chatter, everyone happy and it was decided not to hire a removal truck as it was not far to travel back and forth with a trailer Carl suggested hiring. That would work out much cheaper and there should be enough manpower with his friend Michael. Jonah was sure that Stephan wouldn't mind helping one afternoon. The move should be straight forward with them able to take time to move out and with the house being empty made it easier still.

The solicitors put through the sale and purchase agreements, the mortgage was transferred and they received the keys to the house. Carl couldn't take time off work so the move would happen on the weekend. The weather forecast was for a fine 18 degrees day, Gemma said she would prepare the meals and provide tea, coffee and cake the whole weekend for the workers. It was a happy, exciting time with lots of noise and enthusiasm, all of it was moved in on Saturday except for the contents of the storage container which arrived later in the day.

Sunday was filled with heavy lifting of beds, fridge, freezer and laundry along with the heavy furniture and electrics and possessions that had all been in storage. Although it had only been a few months it was curiously thrilling to have their familiar things back with them again. Sue's favourite comfy dusky pink bedroom chair, her china and clothes that won't fit her at present all started to fill their new home.

The household items in each room of Bradshaw Road, were not all set in their permanent position but quickly put in the room Sue wanted them in for now, with a stack of cardboard boxes still sitting in the centre of the lounge, she would slowly unpack through the week, hanging clothes and filling the kitchen cupboards.

Tired and much quieter, the men finally descended on Gemma's dining room late afternoon for a thank-you of bread rolls, cold chicken, salad and hot pizza Gemma had made, straight out of the oven. There was ample to help themselves, ham and mustard sandwiches, pikelets with jam and cream plus a crystal bowl full of various wrapped chocolates to celebrate the occasion.

Moving house was tiring but wonderful for Sue and Carl, and as Sue remained unable to lift anything she unpacked the cartons and once she had decided on which room each chest of drawers and bookcase were going into, she set about filling them and emptying each box. It was fun and sometimes difficult to decide but that didn't matter, they could change their minds later and move the odd thing around.

The important thing was to have their own bed and belongings around them once more, now married and expecting a baby in their first home was unbelievably wonderful.

It was a mild morning, not even cold when at 5am Sue thought she better not wait any longer, so reaching over she placed a hand on his shoulder.

"Love, I think I need to go to the hospital," she gently shook Carl's shoulder, not wanting to frighten him between the cramping pain waves that kept on coming in her stomach.

Carl jumped half out of his wits, "What?" He was jarred out of a deep sleep. Looking over to Sue he could see her screwed up face, she was in pain.

"Can you help me standup please?" she whispered calmly but nevertheless incapacitated.

"Is the baby coming?" He leapt out of bed this being the day he had been preparing for, pulled on his jeans and tee-shirt, he grabbed for the small, packed bag sitting on her favourite pink chair and rushed for the door, ready to get out the car.

"What about me?" she called impatiently, a little more assertively this time.

"Oh I forgot." He gently pulled her up to sit on the side of the bed, slipping her arm into her dressing gown and sliding her feet into slip-on shoes.

"Are they close together now? Do you think it's time." He stammered.

"Yes, I've been in labour for a couple of hours now and they are getting quite close together. I know its time!" she panted.

After setting her and the bag into the car he carefully reversed out of the garage and they set off to the Waterworth Maternity Hospital. During the drive, the pain came in excruciating waves with short spaces of relief. In between contractions she used her mobile to inform the hospital she was on the way, expecting her first baby. She wasn't worried about the baby being healthy as she only had two weeks to go and the midwife said it was a good size. However, she was dreading giving birth and wished she didn't have to go through the torture to get her baby.

She was lucky that her pregnancy had gone well and she had only finished working six weeks ago, she had been feeling even more energetic and well lately. Gemma had warned her that sometimes you can feel like spring cleaning just before a baby is born, something to do with the hormones making her feel energetic.

She was finding the drive a bit bumpier than she would normally though, and she was anxious to get to the hospital as soon as possible now the extreme cramping in her stomach was crying out for attention.

Carl drove directly up to the doorway, parked in the emergency drop off area that he had previously searched out and viewed online two weeks ago, when Sue had packed her bag in preparation. As he opened the passenger door to help, a nurse rushed over. Sue looked into her eyes in desperate panic.

"Hello Mrs Gibson, we have been expecting you, everything is okey we can take it from here," said the nurse.

She smiled, kindly reassuring Sue as she supported her by hooking her arm under Sue's, while Carl fetched the bag from the back seat. It was a slow awkward walk into a hospital room where she lay back on a bed, relieved to be in hospital with nurses and doctors around.

Carl left the room to catch his breath, it was too early to phone mum and dad and emotions were running high, restlessly pacing around the waiting room wondering what to do with himself.

A nurse peeped in to see him, "Would you like to be in the room during delivery?" she enquired.

"Yes, if that's okey." He rushed over to the room with the lemon painted door where he had left his wife.

"Your wife has said she is okey with it and would like you to be with her," she smiled nodding.

The nightclothes Sue had worn had been replaced and she was now encased in a loose fitting, depersonalized white hospital garment when Carl bent over to kiss her. He stood at the side of the bed, she didn't look too good, he continued to smooth away glistening beads of perspiration from her forehead as time seemed to stand still. The doctor arrived also covered in a white gown, all Carl saw was white everywhere, he couldn't comprehend it.

He was utterly drained at seeing the severe pain his wife was in, and at this new experience that no one could ever prepare for. He kept breathing and consoling his pain ridden wife every time a wave surged and he felt completely helpless.

Thankfully, the doctor entered the room in a hurry and Carl's anxiety was relieved somewhat, as he decided to leave the room while he talked with Sue. Carl had to trust the unfamiliar doctor knew what he was doing.

A few minutes later after examining Sue, the doctor asked the nurse to please bring Mr Gibson back into the room.

"Mr and Mrs Gibson, I'm a little concerned that things are not progressing as fast as I would like, so I'm going to get the mobile Xray unit to take a picture to establish the size of baby's head and the size of your pelvis if that's alright with you both?" he suggested.

"Is something wrong doctor?" Sue beseeched.

"Not at all, everything is fine, baby is being monitored and is doing well but sometimes we need to do a caesarean if the baby looks to be too big. It is best to be prepared and not to risk an emergency situation."

"Yes, you can X-ray if it won't hurt the baby." They both nodded in agreement.

"No, it won't harm the baby, it is often used and carefully measured.

Another contraction subsided and Sue relaxed again dreading the next one she knew was coming. Nervous tension floated in the air making the small room seem suffocatingly smaller, as the portable X-ray trolley was wheeled in.

"I'll just wait outside love," he said and kissed her on the check, amidst fear, worry and desire for the unborn baby to be okey. It all combined to make Carl feel desperate, and unable to do a thing to help his wife and baby, he started to pray.

Carl watched the door of the room re-open as the doctor exited the room and followed the trolley towards a smaller room further down the corridor. He rushed back to Sue's bedside, just as she had a dreadful wave of pain.

"We just wait now I suppose to hear back about what to do next." Carl said looking on, he held her hand giving it an encouraging squeeze.

"Yes, he said he would be right back."
Footsteps sounded on the could vinyl floor as the doctor re-entered the room.

"Good news," he announced loudly. "The measurements show that with a bit of professional help, you will not need a caesarean and we will increase your pain relief with a drug straight into the spinal which is being prepared now for you Mrs Gibson." He smiled.

The nurse re-appeared releasing the brake on the bottom of the bed with her foot creating a clang before it rolled easily.

"We're taking you into the delivery room now and all going well you will have your baby very soon." She smiled.

Carl followed them down the corridor still nervous but accepting that things were happening, progress was being made so the churning desperation and feelings of inadequacy eased a little.

The pain was constant now and watching the glistening beads of perspiration and the sound of extreme agony and physically hard work Carl weakened, he could no longer stand watching his wife struggle.

What was at first a shock pregnancy announcement, had turned into a wonderful surprise with growing acceptance and welcoming of becoming a father, but now at this moment his emotions were totally confused. Carl felt a total lack of understanding of how people could say giving birth was a beautiful thing, his heart was torn, his duty of care and love for both Sue and his unborn child pressing on him unbearable anguish and inadequacy.

He kissed Sue on the lips before leaving, "Your doing well love, nearly there, I'll be back in a minute," he whispered.

Chapter 21

Rushing through the door he headed straight down the corridor towards the toilet door on the right, hung his head over the small porcelain hand basin and swished cold water on his face. With outstretched arms he rested, holding on tightly to each side of the bench space before reaching for a paper towel. He wasn't built for this.

Once he checked in the mirror that he looked okey, he made his way back to the waiting room that he had first been in on arrival at the hospital in the early hours of the morning, unsure of what to do he guiltily sunk down into an armchair. He waited in the dimly lit room, the still dawning of the morning slowly pushing its way into the room, the beginning of a new day. Should he phone his parents yet or wait? Perhaps he could text as he was too shaken to speak anyway.

Pulling his mobile out of his pocket Carl began to send a short text message to mum, letting them know everything was okey Sue was in delivery at the local maternity hospital. After it was sent he switched the phone off again because of hospital policy.

He sat, couldn't read, couldn't really think and couldn't comprehend why he was emotionally exhausted. He definitely wasn't going back into that room again and just watched as a small ray of daylight filtered through the one window in the small waiting room. Then he heard it! A baby was screaming its lungs out, Carls breathing stilled to listen to how the onset quickly settled into little gentle baby snuffles slowly calming down. Just then the nurse popped her head around the door.

"Mr Gibson there you are, congratulations you have a girl, she's a good heathy 6lb 2oz," she smiled. "Would you like to meet your wee girl?"

With his arm gesturing towards the baby sounds he shakenly exclaimed, "What! is that her?" so surprised as he leapt up out of the armchair almost overturning it. "How are they both, is everything okey?" he gasped as he made a dash passed the nurse towards the room.

"Yes, everything is fine, your wife is tired which is to be expected." She pushed open the door and let him enter first.

Suddenly without thinking he automatically started walking softly on tippy toes overwhelmed, he had no idea why.

"Oh love," he carefully bent over the hospital bed to kiss her.

Her face a pale translucent white with sleepy heavy eyelids. Laying on her chest was a softly wrapped up bundle, he could see a wet mass of black hair and an angelic tiny head, with a screwed up face looking out, glistening eyes wide open under dark lashes taking in the world. Then she let out a sound that awakened his senses and shot a protective dagger surging through his veins into his heart, his baby girl had arrived and she was beautiful.

"She's lovely isn't she," Sue murmured.

"She sure is," he replied.

Sweeping the hair off Sue's brow his eyes began to tear up; he quickly blinked to control them. What an amazing moment and time stood still; the three of them a jumble of emotions, happiness, peace and contentment, a myriad of life burst forth in that small room and showered on that little family.

It was 8am when Carl phoned Gemma and Jonah, "We have a little girl," he choked. "They are both doing well."

"That's wonderful," exclaimed Gemma. "Do you have a name picked out yet?"

"We have a couple but haven't decided yet," he said. "I'll see you both later, bye." He didn't want to talk; he wanted to be with his wife and baby.

"Bye son." Gemma switched off the phone to sit and pause with a smile. "We're grandparents," she called to Jonah.

After four days mother and baby settled into home life and with doting grandparents, Sue was able to get the rest she needed to pickup strength and get into a routine. It wasn't long before they started to enjoy the fine days pushing the pram out for a stroll and a visit. Gemma was founding it difficult to walk far now, which didn't matter as Sue welcomed the exercise to get her figure back. Besides, she was so grateful to be able to pop-in for a chat now that she no longer worked. Life had changed so much, being a full time mum was a new challenge to master and Sue appreciated how fortunate she was to have adult company and support just down the road, very aware that so many people didn't have family close by.

Beautiful little Coral also glowed from the love and caring in her life and time raced along perfectly for them all happily enjoying her. Gemma watched as Coral's ebony curls bounced off her small shoulders and her skin was all peaches and cream from the fresh air. She loved to run around grandmas garden, carefully smelling the marigolds and plucking a strawberry from grandads plants as he handed her a small pink cane basket to pick some fruit for the kitchen fruit bowl. She was precious, petite and a well mannered two year old child nurtured with love, kindness and all the time in the world.

Gemma's vertigo never went away and she found it better to give up dancing and to just enjoy her granddaughter. Jonah didn't mind and he spent many hours wandering around and showing Coral the garden, it had become her routine to also help grandad to feed Shed Cat sometimes when she visited. They wandered down to sit on the jetty together when the tide was way out. Coral sat swinging her legs and asking loads of questions which Jonah enjoyed.

"Is that your boat grandad?" she asked looking over at Jonah sitting beside her.

"Yes, but its old and Shed Cat likes to live in it now."

"Can we make a bed for Shed Cat grandad?"

"Yes, why not. I suppose he might like that. I think I have an old box up at the house, lets go and get that," he said amused.

Holding her hand they carefully walked off the green slimy jetty and then she took off running back to the house very excited, rushing inside with the news.

"We're going to make Shed Cat a bed!" she yelled out to anyone who would listen.

Jonah fetched an old wooden apple box from his tool shed, it had been there a while but was clean and sound as Coral ran around animatedly, then they scrounged some soft handtowels from Gran who knew she could buy some more next time she was at the shops. Who was she to say no, to such an important mission. With the towels carefully tucked under her arm Coral scuttled off back to the boat house and Grandad was not far behind. She had grown up knowing not to go near the water, and the shed didn't have any water in it now, only a ramp that slide out the front door and that was always locked.

Jonah helped her into the boat as it wiggled a bit as it sat wedged on the wooden floor. It was a joint effort, finding the best place to lay the box and it was decided to tuck it securely under the seat after Coral filled it with comfy towels. After a bit of fussing and once she was completely happy with it, she then helped to refill the dry biscuit feeder, so Shed Cat always had enough food flowing when he needed it. The plastic feeder was nailed to the wall up off the floor so no vermin could reach the food. They didn't see the cat today but Grandad assured her Shed Cat would find the warm bed later on when the sun went down.

Strolling back to the house they found that hot scones had just come out of the oven, the warm steam rising up from each one as Gemma stacked them onto one of her favourite country cottage China plates.

"Your mum and dad will be back soon to pick you up; they just popped out to get some cream to go with the scones."

Grandma's face was all wrinkled now when she smiled. But she still had a soft kind voice and made yummy scones.

"Do you have any jam to go on them?" Coral asked.

"Yes, you can help find it in the fridge for me if you like."

Jonah had gone to wash his hands and put his slippers on. They all heard the car turn up and Coral helped to set the table for a nice afternoon tea, everyone liked scones, jam and cream and served with a fresh pot of tea made in Grandma's blue floral teapot.

They sat around the table listening to Coral chatter away, she was a lively carefree child and she was enrolled to go to Kindy childcare centre in another six months. The adults sat quietly watching.

"We have some news," said Sue looking at Gemma.

"Oh what's that?" she asked as she helped Coral blob the jam from a teaspoon to rest on the top of a scone.

"I'm pregnant!" she smiled.

"Oh how wonderful, how far along are you?" she and Jonah both enquired loudly together.

"Three months." She reached over to take Carl's hand as he offered it with a proud smile. They looked thrilled to be expecting another child, a little brother or sister for Coral.

"That's fantastic news we're both so pleased for you," said Jonah, whacking Carl on the back. "Well done."

"Coral will be at childcare when I have the baby and you will both be kept busy with her and the new baby as well." Sue piped up.

"Oh, I might be able to help run her to childcare or pick her up." Jonah offered happy to be involved.

They all nodded, it was wonderful family news and feeling overwhelmed Gemma wandered off to the bedroom to sit on the bed contemplating, she wanted to say a quick prayer of thanks.

It was amazing how wonderful her life was now that she was married to the right person. Jonah was a genuine kind soul, a caring person that everyone dreamt of finding. She was so fortunate that she not only had a loyal elderly dog, a daughter-in-law, a beautiful grandchild and also a new family member on the way, a tiny tear slid from the corner of her eye.

Because of her previous unhappy marriage she could appreciate the value of what she now had, she understood that the hurt and pain of losing her husband somehow shrouded her in a dull fog, a cloud that managed to rob her of all zest and enthusiasm for life shared with another person, she had made the best of a bad situation. Those days her laughter existed because of the mutual love she held for her dog and clinging to her faith that she would break free of its hold.

Then along came Jonah, and Gemma encountered the power of perseverance, determination to live, and had seen Jonah's ability to draw on the power of mind to deliver miracles. She sat contemplating on that bad year, remembering the grief and losing him at sea, the dreadful fear of him being in a capsized boat.

They had both found their strength and resilience to discover more than she had ever thought possible.

Jonah appeared in the doorway, he sat down quietly on the bed beside her; without speaking he picked up her hand and rested it in his warm palm as she lay her head on his shoulder, he smiled down into her ocean blue eyes, a thoughtful smile that conveyed more than any words could, he understood she was in awe of her life. Gemma was happy, words were inadequate and not needed, he understood that.

They sat silently holding hands, Gemma knew that what was once a clouded solitary life had somehow slipped into a comfortable routine with Jonah. He and the family filled all of her wonderful days, and they both had an important part to play in the lives of the grandchildren. Each morning rising from bed she looked upon the precious keepsake sitting on the bedside table; the picture of her and Jonah in the silver fillagree picture frame, taken on their cruise before they were married. A joyful smile spread across her face every time she looked at it, a constant reminder of how Jonah's patience and fortitude made her his wife. She was happy and she wouldn't change her life in any way.

Every so often they all enjoyed a family get together over a bar-b-que, sometimes the meat was charred and cooked a little more than she liked, but she didn't care; that unforgettable smell of bar-b-que meat wafted into the outside air and she enjoyed watching two grandchildren run and play in the orchard and garden. Gemma was grateful for the love and bond grown between Jonah and her son from her first marriage, and the affection shown as they worked together, Carl did the cooking and Jonah topped up drinks on a balmy cool evening. Gemma was bursting with joy and gratitude to the Lord for blessing her with this family.

As the years continued to rush past life was good, even down at the boathouse Shed Cat was never alone, a gathering of furry friends also appreciated the shelter and had joined him.

Most days, Jonah and Gemma walked hand in hand down to watch the sun rise over the water and smiled, it was another lovely day and no matter how many they had together or how many challenges, they faced them united and knew they had lived the finest life possible. Jonah and Gemma both discovered the individuals power of positive thinking, and the insurmountable faith she held within her soul kept her strong, steadfast and hopeful. Enduring with determination to find a *happy ever after*, they had both fought and found it.

Have you followed L.J. Bernard

on Facebook?

Keep up to date on Lynette's latest books

by searching Google.

Stay in touch

facebook.com/lynettebernard

Email: authornewsletterljb@gmail.com

About the Author

A New Zealand mother of two.
Lynette has found an outlet for her creativity
and enjoys the freedom of speech by
writing her novels for you all. She hopes that
you are gripped by the emotion and
enjoy the stories.

Lynette happily divides her time between
friends, family, writing and
gardening in the diverse New Zealand
climate.

www.ingramcontent.com/pod-product-compliance
Lightning Source LLC
Chambersburg PA
CBHW022053290426
44109CB00014B/1079